Table of (

Vocabula

MW01515224

Tools

Months, Days, Numbers

Phrases | Notes

Contact through:
info@thelingoguide.com
www.thelingoguide.com

Published by:
The Lingo Guide, LLC
Nashville, TN

This publication may not be reproduced, stored in a retrieval system, or transmitted in whole or in part, in any form or by any means, electronic or mechanical, photocopied, recorded or otherwise, without the prior written permission of The Lingo Guide, LLC. Copyright ©2006 The Lingo Guide, LLC. All rights reserved. v1.4

Dedicated to:
David, Caleb and Silas with love.

Phrase Topics Table of Contents

The Lingo Guide for Builders is meant solely as a tool to assist in advancing communications between English and Spanish speakers. It is not meant to be used for any legally binding communications nor is the editor, publisher, or author responsible for any errors, omissions, or damages resulting from the use of information contained in The Lingo Guide for Builders.

Vocab.

A

access	acceso	*ahk-SEH-soh*
addition	adición	*ah-dee-seeON*
air compressor	compresor de aire	*kohm-preh-SOHR deh EYE-reh*
anchor	ancla	*AHN-klah*
architect	arquitecto	*ahr-key-TECH-toh*
attic	ático, desván	*AH-tee-koh, dehs-VAN*

B

back hoe	retroexcavadora	*reh-troh-ex-kah-vah-DOH-rah*
backfill	relleno	*reh-YEH-noh*
baseboard	zócalo	*SOH-kah-loh*
basement	sótano	*SOH-tah-noh*
bathroom	baño	*BAH-neeoh*
bathtub	bañera	*bah-nee-EH-rah*
battery	batería, pila	*bah-teh-REE-ah, PEE-lah*
bedroom	dormitorio	*door-me-TOH-reeoh*
block, blocking	traba, trabar	*TRAH-bah, trah-BAHR*
	bloque, bloquear	*BLOH-keh, bloh-kehAHR*
board	tabla	*TAH-blah*
brace	abrazadera	*ah-brah-sah-DEH-rah*
	tirante	*tee-RAHN-teh*
bracing	refuerzo	*reh-FWEHR-soh*
brick	ladrillo	*lah-DREE-yoh*
building	edificio	*eh-dee-FEE-seeoh*

C

carpenter	carpintero	*car-peen-TEH-roh*
caulking	enmasillado	*ehn-mah-see-YAH-doh*
ceiling	techo	*TEH-choh*
ceramic floor	piso cerámico	*PEE-soh seh-RAH-me-koh*
ceramic tile	baldosa cerámica	*bahl-DOH-sah seh-RAH-me-kah*
chalk line	línea de marcar	*LEE-neh-ah deh mahr-KAHR*
	tendel	*tehn-DEHL*
	línea de gis	*LEE-neh-ah deh hees*
chase	canaleta	*kah-nah-LEH-tah*
	muesca	*mooEHS-kah*
chimney	chimenea	*chee-meh-NEH-ah*
circuit breaker	interruptor de circuito	*een-teh-rrroop-TOHR deh seer-KWEE-toh*
coarse	grueso, áspero	*groo-EH-soh, AHS-peh-roh*

code	código	*KOH-dee-goh*
code official	autoridad competente	ahoo-toh-tee-DAHD kohm-peh-TEHN-teh
	oficial de códigos	oh-fee-seeAHL deh KOH-dee-gohs
column	columna	*koh-LOOM-nah*
concrete	concreto	*kohn-KREH-toh*
concrete slab	resalto de *concreto*	*reh-SAHL-toh deh kohn-KREH-toh*
conduit	conducto	*kohn-DOOK-toh*
	tubería	*to-beh-REE-ah*
connection	conexión, unión	*koh-nehx-seeON, oo-neeON*
connector	conector	*koh-nehk-TOHR*
contractor	constructor	*kohns-trook-TOHR*
cracked walls	paredes agrietadas	*pah-REH-dehs ah-gree-eh-TAH-dahs*
cracks	rajas, grietas	*RAH-hahs, gree-EH-tahs*
crawl space	sótano	*SOH-tah-noh*
crown	corona (grapas)	*koh-ROH-nah (GRAH-pahs)*
curb	bordillo	*bore-DEE-yoh*
	guarnición	*gwahr-nee-seeON*

D

damper	regulador	*reh-goo-lah-DOOR*
dead end	callejón sin salida	*kah-yeh-HOHN seen sah-LEE-dah*
deck, decking	cubierta (balcón)	*koo-beeEHR-tah (bahl-KOHN)*
design drawings	planos	*PLAH-nohs*
diagonal bracing	soporte diagonal	*soh-PORE-teh dee-ah-goh-NAHL*
dig	excavar	*ex-kah-VAHR*
door	puerta	*pooh-EHR-tah*
doorway	entrada	*ehn-TRAH-dah*
dormer	ventana vertical de buhardilla	*vehn-TAH-nah vehr-tee-KAHL deh boo-ahr-DEE-yah*
	aposento salidizo	*ah-poh-SEHN-toh sah-lee-DEE-soh*
double plate	solera doble	*soh-LEH-rah DOH-bleh*
drain, drainage	desagüe, drenaje	*deh-SAH-gweh, dreh-NAH-heh*
drill, drilling	taladro, taladrar	*tah-LAH-droh, tah-lah-DRAHR*
dry wall	muro en seco	*MOO-roh ehn SEH-koh*
dryer	secadora	*seh-kah-DOH-rah*
duct	conducto	*kohn-DOOK-toh*

Vocab.

dwelling	vivienda	*vee-veeEHN-dah*
	residencia	*reh-see-DEHN-seeah*

E

edge (on edge)	canto	*KAHN-toh*
	(de canto a canto)	*(deh KAHN-toh ah KAHN-toh)*
	borde	*BOHR-deh*
electrical outlet	enchufe	*ehn-CHOO-feh*
electrician	electricista	*eh-lehk-tree-SEES-tah*
electricity	electricidad	*eh-lehk-tree-see-DAHD*
elevator	elevador	*eh-leh-vah-DOOR*
	ascensor	*ah-sehn-SOHR*
embankment	terraplén	*teh-rrrah-PLEHN*
enclose	encerrar	*ehn-seh-RRRAHR*
enclosed	encerrado	*ehn-seh-RRRAH-doh*
enclosure	cerramiento	*seh-rrrah-meEHN-toh*
encompass	incluir	*een-clue-EER*
enforce	hacer cumplir	*ah-SEHR koom-PLEER*
engineer	ingeniero	*een-heh-neeEH-roh*
exhaust	escape	*ehs-KAH-peh*
	extracción	*ex-trak-seeON*
exhaust fan	ventilador de	*vehn-tee-lah-DOOR deh*
	extracción	*ex-trak-seeON*
exit	salida	*sah-LEE-dah*
expansion bolt	perno	*PEHR-noh*
	tornillo de	*tohr-NEE-yoh deh*
	expansión	*ex-pahn-seeON*
expansion joint	junta de	*HOON-tah deh*
	dilatación/	*dee-lah-tah-seeON/*
	expansión	*ex-pahn-seeON*
extension cord	cable de	*KAH-bleh deh*
	extensión	*ex-ten-seeON*
exterior wall	muro	*MOO-roh*
	pared exterior	*pah-REHD ex-teh-reeOHR*
exterior/	superficie	*soo-pehr-FEE-see-eh*
interior surface	interna/externa	*een-TEHR-nah/ex-TEHR-nah*

F

façade	fachada	*fah-CHAH-dah*
facing brick	ladrillo frontal	*lah-DREE-yoh frohn-TAHL*
fan	abanico	*ah-BAH-nee-koh*
	ventilador	*vehn-tee-lah-DOOR*

Vocab

fastener	sujetador	*soo-heh-tah-DOOR*
faucet	llave, grifo	*YAH-veh, GREE-foh*
felt	fieltro	*fee-EHL-troh*
fence	cerca	*SEHR-kah*
filled	relleno, rellenado	*reh-YEH-noh, reh-yeh-NAH-doh*
finish, finished	acabado	*ah-kah-BAH-doh*
finishing nail	clavo sin cabeza	*KLAH-voh seen kah-BEH-sah*
fire alarm	alarma de incendios	*ah-LAHR-mah deh een-SEHN-deeohs*
fire department	cuerpo de bomberos	*KWEHR-poh deh bohm-BEH-rohs*
first floor	primer piso	*pree-MEHR PEE-soh*
fitting	accesorio	*ahk-seh-SOH-reeoh*
	conexión	*koh-nehx-seeON*
fixture	artefacto	*ahr-teh-FAHK-toh*
	accesorio	*ahk-seh-SOH-reeoh*
flashing	cubrejuntas	*koo-breh-HOON-tahs*
	tapajuntas	*tah-pah-HOON-tahs*
flashlight	linterna	*lean-TEHR-nah*
	lámpara	*LAHM-pah-rah*
flex conduit	conducto portacables flexible	*kohn-DOOK-toh pore-tah-KAH-blehs flehx-EE-bleh*
floodlight	iluminación industrial	*ee-loo-me-nah-seeON een-doos-treeAHL*
	luz de faro	*loose deh FAH-roh*
floor	piso	*PEE-soh*
floor deck	plataforma	*plah-tah-FOR-mah*
flooring	revestimiento para pisos	*reh-vehs-tee-meEHN-toh PAH-rah PEE-sohs*
	material para pisos	*mah-teh-reAHL PAH-rah PEE-sohs*
flue	conducto de humo	*kohn-DOOK-toh deh OO-moh*
fluorescent	fluorescente	*flue-oh-reh-SEHN-teh*
footing	cimiento	*see-meEHN-toh*
	sobrestante	*soh-brehs-TAHN-teh*
foreman	supervisor	*soo-pehr-vee-SOHR*
forms (concrete)	encofrados	*ehn-koh-FRAH-dohs*
formwork	encofrado	*ehn-koh-FRAH-doh*

foundation	fundación	foon-dah-seeON
foundation sill plate	placa de solera de fundación	PLAH-kah deh soh-LEH-rah deh foon-dah-seeON
foundation walls	muros de fundación	MOO-rohs deh foon-dah-seeON
frame	marco	MAHR-koh
	estructura	ehs-trook-TO-rah
	armazón	ahr-mah-ZOHN
frame, door/window	marco (bastidor) de puerta/ventana	MAHR-koh (bahs-tee DOOR) deh pooh-EHR-tah/ vehn-TAH-nah
framed	armado	ahr-MAH-doh
framework	armazón	ahr-mah-SOHN
framing	estructura	ehs-trook-TO-rah
fumes	gases	GAH-sehs
furred out, furring	enrasado	ehn-rah-SAH-doh
fuse	fusibles	foo-SEE-blehs
fuse box	caja de fusibles	KAH-hah deh foo-SEE-blehs

G

gable	hastial	ahs-teAHL
gable roof	techo a dos aguas	TEH-choh ah dohs AH-gwahs
gage/gauge (thickness)	calibre	kah-LEE-breh
garage	garaje	gah-RAH-heh
	cochera	koh-CHEH-rah
garbage disposal	triturador de basura	tree-to-rah-DOOR deh bah-SOO-rah
gasket	arandela	ah-rahn-DEH-lah
	empaque	ehm-PAH-keh
	junta	HOON-tah
gas main	cañería principal de gas	kah-nee-eh-REE-ah preen-see-PAHL deh gahs
gage/gauge (instrument)	calibrador	kah-lee-brah-DOOR
	indicador	een-dee-kah-DOOR
girder	viga	VEE-gah
glazed, glazing	vidriado	vee-dree-AH-doh
	encristalado	ehn-krees-tah-LAH-doh
glue	resistol	reh-sees-TOHL
	pegamento	peh-gah-MEHN-toh
grade	nivel de terreno	NEE-vehl deh teh-RRREH-noh
grade (ground elevation)	inclinación	een-klee-nah-seeON

granite	granito	*GRAH-nee-toh*
gravel	grava, gravilla	*GRAH-vah, grah-VEE-yah*
grille	reja, rejilla	*REH-hah, reh-HE-yah*
grommet	arandela, ojal	*ah-rahn-DEH-lah, oh-HAL*
ground fault circuit	interruptor fusible	*een-teh-rrroop-TOHR foo-SEE-bleh*
	de seguridad	*deh seh-goo-ree-DAHD*
	a tierra	*ah teeEH-rrrah*
ground level	planta baja	*PLAHN-tah BAH-hah*
ground wire	cable a tierra	*KAH-bleh ah teeEH-rrrah*
grout	lechada/mortero	*leh-CHAH-dah/more-TEH-roh*
	de cemento	*deh seh-MEHN-toh*
guest	invitado	*een-vee-TAH-doh*
gutter	canal	*kah-NAHL*
	canaleta	*kah-nah-LEH-tah*
gypsum board	tablero de yeso	*tah-BLEH-roh deh YEH-soh*
	panel de yeso	*PAH-nehl deh YEH-soh*
	plancha de yeso	*PLAHN-chah deh YEH-soh*
	plafón de yeso	*plah-FOHN deh YEH-soh*

H

hallway	pasillo	*pah-SEE-yoh*
handicapped	discapacitado	*dees-kah-pah-see-TAH-doh*
	minusválido	*me-noos-VAH-lee-doh*
handle	manija	*mah-NEE-hah*
	mango	*MAHN-goh*
	agarradera	*ah-gah-rrrah-DEH-rah*
handling	manipulación	*mah-nee-pooh-lah-seeON*
handrail	pasamanos	*pah-sah-MAH-nohs*
hangers	ganchos	*GAHN-chohs*
	colgaderos	*kohl-gah-DEH-rohs*
hardboard	tablero duro	*tah-BLEH-roh DO-roh*
hatch	compuerta	*kohm-pooh-EHR-tah*
hazard	peligro	*peh-LEE-groh*
hazardous	peligroso, dañino	*peh-lee-GROH-soh, dah-NEE-noh*
header	cabecera	*kah-beh-SEH-rah*
	cabezal	*kah-beh-SAHL*
heater	calefactor	*kah-leh-fahk-TOHR*
	calentador	*kah-lehn-tah-DOOR*
heating	calefacción	*kah-leh-fahk-seeON*
hinge	bisagra	*bee-SAH-grah*

Vocab.

hip	lima	*LEE-mah*
	lima hoya	*LEE-mah OH-yah*
	lima tesa	*LEE-mah TEH-sah*
hip roof	techo a cuatro aguas	*TEH-choh ah KWAH-troh AH-gwahs*
hip tile	teja para limas	TEH-hah PAH-rah LEE-mahs
hole	hoyo	*OH-yoh*
	agujero	*ah-goo-HEH-roh*
	boquete	*boh-KEH-teh*
	hueco	*WEH-koh*
hood	campana	*kahm-PAH-nah*
(chimney/kitchen)	(chimenea/ cocina)	*(chee-meh-NEH-ah/ koh-SEE-nah)*
hose	manguera	*mahn-GEH-rah*
hose threads	rosca de manguera	*ROHS-kah deh mahn-GEH-rah*
hot water	agua caliente	*AH-gwah kah-lee-EHN-teh*
HVAC	calefacción	*kah-leh-fahk-seeON*
	ventilación	*vehn-tee-lah-seeON*
	aire acondicionado	EYE-reh *ah-kohn-dee-seeoh-NAH-doh*

I

incline	declive	*deh-KLEE-veh*
	inclinación	*een-klee-nah-seeON*
	pendiente	*pehn-deeEHN-teh*
	inclinar	*een-klee-NAHR*
	ladear	*lah-deh-AHR*
inspector	inspector	*eens-pehk-TOHR*
	supervisor	*soo-pehr-vee-SOHR*
insulating	aislante	*eyes-LAHN-teh*
insulation	aislamiento	*eyes-lah-meEHN-toh*
	aislante	*eyes-LAHN-teh*
interior room	cuarto interior	*KWAHR-toh een-teh-reeOHR*
interlocking	enclavamiento	*ehn-klah-vah-meEHN-toh*
	entrelazado	*ehn-treh-lah-SAH-doh*

J

jobsite	lugar de la obra/ en obra	*loo-GAHR deh lah OH-brah/ ehn OH-brah*
joint	unión	*oo-neeON*
joint compound	pasta de muro	*PAHS-tah deh MOO-roh*
joist	vigueta	*vee-GEH-tah*

joist, floor	vigueta del piso	*vee-GEH-tah dehl PEE-soh*
joist hanger	estribo para vigueta	*ehs-TREE-boh PAH-rah vee-GEH-teh*
junction	empalme, unión	*ehm-PAHL-meh, oo-neeON*
junction box	caja de conexiones	*KAH-hah deh koh-nehx-seeOH-nehs*

K

key	llave	*YAH-veh*
keystone	clave	*KLAH-veh*
kitchen	cocina	*koh-SEE-nah*
kitchen stove	estufa	*ehs-TO-fah*
kitchen sink	fregadero	*freh-gah-DEH-roh*
knockout	agujero ciego	*ah-goo-HEH-roh seeEH-goh*

L

ladder	escalera	*ehs-kah-LEH-rah*
landing (stair)	descanso de escaleras	*dehs-KAHN-soh deh ehs-kah-LEH-rahs*
lap siding	revestimiento de tablas con traslapo/solapo	*reh-vehs-tee-meEHN-toh deh TAH-blahs kohn trahs-LAH-poh/soh-LAH-poh*
latch	cerrojo	*seh-RRROH-hoh*
latching device	dispositivo de traba	*dees-poh-see-TEE-voh deh TRAH-bah*
lawn	césped	*SEHS-pehd*
	pasto	*PAHS-toh*
layout	croquis	*kroh-KEYS*
	diseño	*dee-SEH-neeoh*
ledger	travesaño	*trah-veh-SAH-neeoh*
	solera	*soh-LEH-rah*
lift	levantamiento	*leh-vahn-tah-meEHN-toh*
	alzada	*ahl-SAH-dah*
light bulb	bombilla	*bohm-BEE-yah*
light fixture	artefacto de iluminación	*ahr-teh-FAHK-toh deh ee-loo-me-nah-seeON*
limestone	caliza	*kah-LEE-sah*
lining	recubrimiento	*reh-koo-bree-meEHN-toh*
	revestimiento	*reh-vehs-tee-meEHN-toh*
link, linkage	enlace	*ehn-LAH-seh*
	tirante	*tee-RAHN-teh*
	conexión	*koh-nehx-seeON*

lintel	dintel	DEEN-tehl
live load	carga viva	KAHR-gah VEE-vah
load-bearing joist	viga de carga	VEE-gah deh KAHR-gah
loaded area	área cargada	AH-reh-ah kahr-GAH-dah
	área sometida	AH-reh-ah soh-meh-TEE-dah
	a carga	ah KAHR-gah
lock	candado	kahn-DAH-doh
	cerradura	seh-rrrah-DO-rah
	cerrojo	seh-RRROH-hoh
lock bolts	pernos de	PEHR-nohs deh
	seguridad	seh-goo-ree-DAHD
lot	terreno, lote	teh-RRREH-noh, LOH-teh
lumber	madera de	mah-DEH-rah deh
	construcción	kohns-trook-seeON

mailbox	buzón	boo-SOHN
main	principal	preen-see-PAHL
	matriz	mah-TREES
main breaker	interruptor	een-teh-rrroop-TOHR
	principal	preen-see-PAHL
main power cable	cable principal	KAH-bleh preen-see-PAHL
main vent	ventilador	vehn-tee-lah-DOOR
	principal	preen-see-PAHL
mall	centro comercial	SEHN-troh koh-mehr-seeAHL
manhole	boca de acceso	BOH-kah deh ahk-SEH-soh
	pozo de entrada	POH-soh deh ehn-TRAH-dah
mansion	mansión	mahn-seeON
marble	mármol	MAHR-mohl
mason	albañil	ahl-bah-NEE-eel
masonry	mampostería	mahm-pohs-teh-REE-ah
mastic	mastique	mahs-TEEK
measuring tape	cinta de medir	SEEN-tah deh meh-DEEHR
metal deck	plataforma	plah-tah-FOR-mah
	metálica	meh-TAH-lee-kah
metal flagpole	mástil metálico	MAHS-teel meh-TAH-lee-koh
metal roof covering	cubierta metálica	koo-beEHR-tah meh-TAH-lee-kah
	para tejado	PAH-rah teh-HAH-doh
meter	medidor	meh-dee-DOOR
molding	moldura	mohl-DO-rah

mortar	mortero,	mohr-TEH-roh
	argamasa,	ahr-gah-MAH-sah
	mezcla	MEHS-klah
mortise	ranura	*rah-NOO-rah*
mullion (door)	larguero central	*lahr-GEH-roh sehn-TRAHL*

N

nailing strip	listón para clavar	*lees-TOHN PAH-rah klah-VAHR*
nails	clavos	*KLAH-vohs*
neutral wire	cable neutral	*KAH-bleh neh-oo-TRAHL*
nosings	vuelos	*VVEH-lohs*
nuisance	perjuicio	*pehr-hooEE-see-oh*

O

occupancy	capacidad	*kah-pah-see-DAHD*
	ocupación	*oh-koo-pah-seeON*
	cupo	*KOO-poh*
offset	desplazamiento	*dehs-plah-sah-meEHN-toh*
	pieza en "S"	*peeEH-sah ehn EH-seh*
	pieza de inflexión	*peeEH-sah deh een-flehk-seeON*
	desvío	*dehs-VEE-oh*
open air	aire libre	*EYE-reh LEE-breh*
opening	abertura	*ah-behr-TO-rah*
outlet box	caja de enchufe	*KAH-hah deh ehn-CHOO-feh*
	tomacorriente	*toh-mah-koh-rrree-EHN-teh*
overhang	voladizo	*voh-lah-DEE-soh*
	vuelo	*VVEH-loh*
	saledizo	*sah-leh-DEE-soh*
overhaul	reparación	*reh-pah-rah-seeON*
	reparar	*reh-PAH-rahr*
overlap	traslape	*trahs-LAH-peh*
	sobresolape	*soh-breh-soh-LAH-peh*
	superposición	*soo-pehr-poh-see-seeON*
override	cancelar	*kahn-seh-LAHR*
	anular	*ah-noo-LAHR*
overturning	vuelco	*VVEHL-koh*
	volteo	*vohl-TEH-oh*
oxidizers	oxidantes	*ohk-see-DAHN-tehs*

P

pallet	estante	*ehs-TAHN-teh*
	tarima	*tah-REE-mah*
	plataforma	*plah-tah-FOR-mah*

paint	pintura	*peen-TO-rah*
painter	pintor	*peen-TOHR*
paneling	empanelado	*ehm-pah-neh-LAH-doh*
particleboard	madera	*mah-DEH-rah*
	aglomerada	*ah-gloh-meh-RAH-dah*
partition	tabique	*tah-BEE-keh*
	separación	*seh-pah-rah-seeON*
	división	*dee-vee-seeON*
passageway	pasillo	*pah-SEE-yoh*
pavement	pavimento	*pah-vee-MEHN-toh*
performance	desempeño	*deh-sehm-PEH-neeoh*
	comportamiento	*kohm-pohr-tah-meEHN-toh*
	rendimiento	*rehn-dee-meEHN-toh*
perlite	perlita	*pehr-LEE-tah*
permit	permiso	pehr-MEE-soh
	(de construcción)	*(deh kohns-trook-seeON)*
piles (footing)	pilotes	*pee-LOH-tehs*
	montones	*mohn-TOH-nehs*
pipe, piping	cañería, caño	*kah-nee-eh-REE-ah, KAH-neeoh*
	tubería, tubo	to-beh-REE-ah, TO-boh
plank	tablón	*tah-BLOHN*
plaster	azotado	*ah-soh-TAH-doh*
	enjarre	*ehn-HAH-rrreh*
	enlucido	*ehn-loo-SEE-doh*
	yeso	*YEH-soh*
plastering	revoque	*reh-VOH-keh*
	enlucido	*ehn-loo-SEE-doh*
	repello	*reh-PEH-yoh*
	forjado	*fohr-HAH-doh*
plastic insulator	aislante plástico	*eyes-LAHN-teh PLAHS-tee-koh*
plug (water)	tapón	*tah-POHN*
plug (electrical)	clavija	*klah-VEE-hah*
	enchufe	*ehn-CHOO-feh*
plumber	fontanero	*fohn-tah-NEH-roh*
	plomero	*ploh-MEH-roh*
plumbing	cañería	*kah-nee-eh-REE-ah*
	tubería	to-beh-REE-ah
	plomería	*ploh-meh-REE-ah*
plumbing fixture	artefacto de	*ahr-teh-FAHK-toh deh*
	sanitario	*sah-nee-TAH-reeoh*
plunger	destapacaños	*dehs-tah-pah-KAH-neeohs*

Vocab.

plywood	tableros de madera contrachapada	*tah-BLEH-rohs deh mah-DEH-rah kohn-trah-chah-PAH-dah*
poles, posts	postes	*POHS-tehs*
portable	portátil	*pore-TAH-teel*
power doors	puertas mecánicas	*pooh-EHR-tahs meh-KAH-nee-kahs*
power outlet	tomacorriente enchufe	*toh-mah-koh-rrree-EHN-teh ehn-CHOO-feh*
power strip	zapatilla eléctrica	*sah-pah-TEE-yah eh-LEHK-tree-kah*
power supply	fuente de alimentación eléctrica	*FWEHN-teh deh ah-lee-mehn-tah-seeON eh-LEHK-tree-kah*
premises	local, sitio	*loh-KAHL, SEE-teeoh*
pressure	presión	*preh-seeON*
primed	imprimado	*eem-pree-MAH-doh*
primer	imprimador	*eem-pree-mah-DOOR*
private	privado	*pree-VAH-doh*
property	propiedad	*proh-pee-eh-DAHD*
property line	línea/límite de propiedad	*LEE-neh-ah/LEE-me-teh deh proh-pee-eh-DAHD*
public safety	seguridad pública	*seh-goo-ree-DAHD POO-blee-kah*
pump	bomba	*BOHM-bah*

R

rack	cremallera	*kreh-mah-YEH-rah*
	tarima	*tah-REE-mah*
rafter	cabria, viga	*KAH-bree-ah, VEE-gah*
rail	carril, baranda	*kah-RRREEL, bah-RAHN-dah*
railing	barandal	*bah-rahn-DAHL*
rate	proporción	*proh-pore-seeON*
rating	clasificación	*klah-see-fee-kah-seeON*
ratio	relación, cociente coeficiente	*reh-lah-seeON, koh-seeEHN-teh co-eh-fee-seeEHN-teh*
rebar	barra de refuerzo	*BAH-rrrah deh reh-FWEHR-soh*
redwood	madera de secoya	*mah-DEH-rah deh seh-KOH-yah*
refuge area	área de refugio	*AH-reh-ah deh reh-FOO-hee-oh*
region	región, tramo	*reh-heeON, TRAH-moh*
register	rejilla	*reh-HE-yah*
	registro	*reh-HES-troh*
regulator	regulador	*reh-goo-lah-DOOR*

Vocab.

reinforced masonry	mampostería reforzada	*mahm-pohs-teh-REE-ah reh-fohr-SAH-dah*
reinforcement	refuerzo	*reh-FWEHR-soh*
	armadura	*ahr-mah-DO-rah*
release	descarga	*dehs-CAR-gah*
	liberación	*lee-beh-rah-seeON*
	desenganche	*des-ehn-GAHN-cheh*
relief valve	válvula/llave de alivio	*VAHL-voo-lah/YAH-veh deh ah-LEE-veeoh*
removal	eliminación	*eh-lee-me-nah-seeON*
	remoción	*reh-moh-seeON*
repair	reparación	*reh-pah-rah-seeON*
reports	informes	*een-FOR-mehs*
	reportes	*reh-PORE-tehs*
residence	residencia	*reh-see-DEHN-seeah*
restroom	baño, sanitario (WC)	*BAH-neeoh, sah-nee-TAH-reeoh (doh-bleh-OO seh)*
rib	costilla	*kohs-TEE-yah*
ridge	cresta, cumbrera	*KREHS-tah, koom-BREH-rah*
ridge board	tabla de cumbrera	*tah-blah de koom-BREH-rah*
rim	borde	*BOHR-deh*
ring shank nail	clavos con fuste corrugado	*KLAH-vohs kohn FOOS-steh koh-rrroo-GAH-doh*
riser (pipe)	tubo vertical	*TO-boh vehr-tee-KAHL*
riser (stair)	contrahuella	kohn-trah-GWEH-yah
rivet	remache	*reh-MAH-cheh*
rock	roca, piedra	*ROH-kah, pee-EH-drah*
roof	tejado	*teh-HAH-doh*
roof covering	revestimiento de tejado	*reh-vehs-tee-meEHN-toh deh teh-HAH-doh*
roof deck	cubierta de tejado	*koo-bee-EHR-tah deh teh-HAH-doh*
roof drain	desagüe de tejado	*deh-SAH-gweh deh teh-HAH-doh*
roof (flat)	tejado plano	*teh-HAH-doh PLAH-noh*
roof sheeting	entarimado de tejado	*ehn-tah-ree-MAH-doh deh teh-HAH-doh*
roof (sloped)	tejado en pendiente	*teh-HAH-doh ehn pehn-dee-EHN-teh*
roofing	techado	*teh-CHAH-doh*
roofing square	cuadro de cubierta de tejado	*KWAH-droh deh koo-be-EHR-tah deh teh-HAH-doh*

room	cuarto	*KWAHR-toh*
	sala	*SAH-lah*
	habitación	*ah-bee-tah-seeON*
rough-in	instalación en	*eens-tah-lah-seeON ehn*
	obra negra/	*OH-brah NEH-grah/*
	gruesa	*groo-EH-sah*
rubbish	basura	*bah-SOO-rah*
rubble	escombro	*ehs-KOHM-broh*
runners	largueros	*lahr-GEH-rohs*

S

sand	arena	*ah-REH-nah*
sandstone	arenisca	*ah-reh-NEES-kah*
sawn timber	maderas	*mah-DEH-rahs*
	aserradas	*ah-seh-RRRAH-dahs*
sawtooth	diente de sierra	*deeEHN-teh deh seeEH-rrrah*
scaffold	andamio	*ahn-DAH-meoh*
schedule,	andamiaje	*ahn-dah-meAH-heh*
scaffolding		
scope	alcance	*ahl-KAHN-seh*
screw	tornillo	*tohr-NEE-yoh*
screwdriver	destornillador	*dehs-tohr-nee-yah-DOOR*
sealant	sellador	*seh-yah-DOOR*
seasoned wood	madera	*mah-DEH-rah*
	estacionada	*ehs-tah-see-oh-NAH-dah*
self-closing	auto cierre	*AHoo-toh seeEH-rrreh*
self-tapping screw	tornillo	*tohr-KNEE-yoh*
	autorroscante	*ahoo-toh-rrrohs-KAHN-teh*
setback	retraso	*reh-TRAH-soh*
sewage	aguas negras	*AH-gwahs NEH-grahs*
	cloacas	*kloh-AH-kahs*
sewer	cloaca	*kloh-AH-kah*
	alcantarilla	*ahl-kahn-tah-REE-yah*
shaft	recinto	*reh-SEEN-toh*
shake, wood	teja de madera	*TEH-hah deh mah-DEH-rah*
	ripia	*REE-pee-ah*
sheathing	entablado	*ehn-tah-BLAH-doh*
sheet	pliego	*pleeEH-goh*
	chapa	*CHAH-pah*
	plancha	*PLAHN-chah*
	lámina	*LAH-me-nah*

Vocab.

sheet metal	lámina/chapa metálica	*LAH-me-nah/CHAH-pah meh-TAH-lee-kah*
	laminado	*lah-me-NAH-doh*
shelf	repisa	*reh-PEE-sah*
shingle	teja, tejamanil	*TEH-hah, teh-hah-mah-NEEL*
shingle, asphalt	teja de asfalto	*TEH-hah deh ahs-FAHL-toh*
shingle, wood	ripio	*REE-pee-oh*
shiplap	traslape/rebajo a media madera	*trahs-LAH-peh/reh-BAH-hoh ah MEH-dee-ah mah-DEH-rah*
shop	taller	*tah-YEHR*
shower door	puerta de ducha	*pooh-EHR-tah deh DO-chah*
shower stall	ducha	*DO-chah*
shower head	regadera	*reh-gah-DEH-rah*
shrinkage	contracción	*kohn-trahk-seeON*
	encogimiento	*ehn-koh-he-meeEHN-toh*
	reducción	*reh-dook-seeON*
shutoff valves	válvulas de cierre	*VAHL-voo-lahs deh seeEH-rrreh*
sidewalk	acera, banqueta	*ah-SEH-rah, bahn-KEH-tah*
sill	soporte	*soh-PORE-teh*
sill plate	solera inferior	*soh-LEH-rah EEN-feh-ree-ohr*
sink	lavabo	*lah-VAH-boh*
site	sitio	*SEE-teeoh*
skylight	tragaluz	*trah-gah-LOOSE*
	claraboya	*klah-rah-BOH-yah*
skyscraper	rascacielos	*rahs-kah-seeEH-lohs*
slab	losa	*LOH-sah*
slate shingle	teja de pizarra	*TEH-hah deh pee-SAH-rrrah*
	durmiente	*doohr-meeEHN-teh*
sleeve	camisa	*kah-ME-sah*
	manga	*MAHN-gah*
sliding doors	puertas corredizas/ deslizantes	*pooh-EHR-tahs koh-rrrreh-DEE-sahs/ dehs-lee-SAHN-tehs*
sliding windows	ventanas corredizas/ deslizantes	*vehn-TAH-nahs co-rrrreh-DEE-sahs/ dehs-lee-SAHN-tehs*
slope	pendiente	*pehn-dee-EHN-teh*
	talud	*tah-LOOD*
	declive	*deh-KLEE-veh*
slump	asentatmiento	*ah-sehn-tah-meEHN-toh*

Vocab.

smoke	humo	*OO-moh*
smoke detector	sensor de humo	*sen-SOHR deh OO-moh*
	detector de humo	*deh-tehk-TOHR deh OO-moh*
soffit	sofito	*soh-FEE-toh*
soil pipe	tubo de aguas negras	*TO-boh deh AH-gwahs NEH-grahs*
sole plate	placa de base	*PLAH-kah de BAH-seh*
span	vano	*VAH-noh*
	claro	KLAH-*roh*
spigot	llave	*YAH-veh*
	grifo	*GREE-foh*
	canilla	*kah-NEE-yah*
	espiga	*ehs-PEE-gah*
spike	clavo para madera	*KLAH-voh PAH-rah mah-DEH-rah*
spiral stairs	escaleras de caracol	*ehs-kah-LEH-rahs deh kah-rah-KOHL*
splice	empalme	*ehm-PAHL-meh*
	traslape	*trahs-LAH-peh*
	junta	HOON-*tah*
	unión	*oo-neeON*
splined	acanalado	*ah-kah-nah-LAH-doh*
spot mopped	adherido en secciones	*ah-deh-REE-doh ehn sehk-seeOH-nehs*
spring	resorte	*reh-SOHR-teh*
sprinkler	rociador	*roh-seeAH-door*
stack	tubería vertical	*to-beh-REE-ah vehr-tee-KAHL*
	tubo vertical	*TO-boh vehr-tee-KAHL*
stack vent	tubería de ventilador	*to-beh-REE-ah deh vehn-tee-lah-DOOR*
stairs/stairway	escaleras	*ehs-kah-LEH-rahs*
steel	acero	*ah-SEH-roh*
steel framing	estructura de acero	*ehs-trook-too-RAH deh ah-SEH-roh*
steeple	campanario	*kahm-pah-NAH-reeoh*
steps	escalones	*ehs-kah-LOH-nehs*
stone	piedra	*pee-EH-drah*
	roca	*ROH-kah*
stress	esfuerzo	*ehs-FWEHR-soh*
strip	listón	*lees-TOHN*

stripping	tiras metálicas	*TEE-rahs meh-TAH-lee-kahs*
structure	estructura	*ehs-trook-TO-rah*
stucco	revoque	*reh-VOH-keh*
	enlucido	*ehn-loo-SEE-doh*
	estuco	*ehs-TO-koh*
stud	montante	*mohn-TAHN-teh*
	parante	*pah-RAHN-teh*
	barrote	*bah-RRROH-teh*
stud bearing wall	muro con	MÖÖ-roh kohn
	montante/	mohn-TAHN-teh/
	parante	pah-RAHN-teh
stud finder	buscador de	*boos-kah-DOOR deh*
	montantes	*mohn-TAHN-tehs*
	busca montantes	BOOS-kah mohn-TAHN-tehs
subfloor	contrapiso	kohn-*trah-PEE-soh*
	bajopiso	*bah-hoh-PEE-soh*
subroof	base de tejado	BAH-seh deh teh-HAH-doh
superintendent	superintendente	soo-pehr-*een-tehn-DEHN-teh*
supervisor	supervisor	soo-pehr-vee-SOHR
	inspector	eens-pehk-TOHR
support	apoyo	*ah-POH-yoh*
	soporte	*soh-PORE-teh*
swinging door	puerta pivotante	pooh-EHR-tah pee-voh-TAHN-teh
switch	interruptor	een-teh-rrroop-TOHR
	apagador	*ah-pah-gah-DOOR*
switch plate	placa de	PLAH-kah deh
	interruptor	een-teh-rrroop-TOHR

T

tag	etiqueta	eh-*tee-KEH-tah*
tar paper	papel de brea	PAH-pehl deh BREH-ah
temporary	provisional	proh-vee-seeoh-NAHL
tension	tensión	ten-seeON
termite	termita	tehr-ME-tah
threshold	umbral	OOM-brahl
tie	amarra	*ah-MAH-rrrah*
	ligadura	lee-GAH-do-rah
	tirante	tee-RAHN-teh
tile (roof)	teja	TEH-hah
tile (floor)	azulejo	*ah-soo-LEH-hoh*
	baldosa	bahl-DOH-sah

tile (masonry)	ladrillo cerámico	*lah-DREE-yoh seh-RAH-me-koh*
timber	madera	*mah-DEH-rah*
toeboard	tabla de pie	*TAH-blah deh PEE-eh*
toenail	clavo oblícuo	*KLAH-voh oh-BLEE-koo-oh*
toilet	sanitario	*sah-nee-TAH-ree-oh*
	excusado	*ex-koo-SAH-doh*
	retrete	*reh-TREH-teh*
tongue and groove	machilhembrado	*mah-cheel-ehm-BRAH-doh*
tools	herramientas	*eh-rrrah-meEHN-tahs*
tread (stair)	huella	*GWEH-yah*
	peldaño	*pehl-DAH-neeoh*
treated wood	madera tratada	*mah-DEH-rah trah-TAH-dah*
trim	molduras	*mohl-DO-rahs*
truss	cercha	*SEHR-chah*
	rcticulado	*reh-tee-koo-LAH-doh*
	armadura	*ahr-mah-DO-rah*
	cabreada	*kah-breh-ah-DAH*
	caballete	kah-bah-YEH-teh
turned-down	zapatillas	*sah-pah-TEE-yahs*
footings	invertidas	*een-vehr-TEE-dahs*

U

underlayment	capa base	*KAH-pah BAH-seh*
	bajo piso	*BAH-hoh PEE-soh*
urinal	urinal	*oo-ree-NAHL*
	urinario	*oo-ree-NAH-reeoh*
	mingitorio	*mean-he-TOH-reeoh*
use	uso	OO-soh
	utilizar	*oo-tee-lee-SAHR*

V

vacuum	vacío	*vah-SEE-oh*
	aspiradora	*ahs-pee-rah-DOH-rah*
value	valor	*vah-LOHR*
vent	respiradero	*rehs-pee-rah-DEH-roh*
	ventilador	*vehn-tee-lah-DOOR*
vestibule	vestíbulo	*vehs-TEE-boo-loh*
vinyl siding	revestimiento de	*reh-vehs-tee-meEHN-toh deh*
	vinilo	*vee-NEE-loh*
vise	morsa	MORE-sah
voltage	voltaje	*vohl-TAH-heh*
volts	voltios	VOHL-teeohs

W

wainscot/	friso	FREE-soh
wainscoting	alfarje	ahl-FAHR-heh
	revestimiento	reh-vehs-tee-meEHN-toh
walking surface	superficie	soo-pehr-FEE-see-eh
walkway	camino	kah-ME-noh
wall	muro	MOO-roh
	pared	PAH-red
wallboard	plancha de yeso	PLAHN-chah de YEH-soh
	cartón de yeso	car-TOHN de YEH-soh
washer and drier	lavadora y secadora	lah-vah-DOH-rah ee seh-kah-DOH-rah
washer	arandela	ah-rahn-DEH-lah
	planchuela de perno	plan-choo-EH-lah deh PEHR-noh
water heater	calentador	kah-lehn-TAH-door
	boiler	boiler
water main	tubería principal/ matriz	to-beh-REE-ah preen-see-PAHL mah-TREES
wax seal	empaque de cera	ehm-PAH-keh deh SEH-rah
weeds	yerbas	YEHR-bahs
welding	soldadura	sohl-dah-DO-rah
window	ventana	vehn-TAH-nah
window sill	soporte de ventana	soh-PORE-teh deh vehn-TAH-nah
	repisa	reh-PEE-sah
wire	alambre	ah-LAHM-breh
wire connectors	conectores de alambre	koh-nehk-TOH-rehs deh ah-LAHM-breh
wire mesh	tela metálica	TEH-lah meh-TAH-lee-kah
wire tie	alambre de paca	ah-LAHM-breh deh PAH-kah
wood framing	bastidores de madera	bahs-tee-DOH-rehs deh mah-DEH-rah
wood shingles	tejas de madera	TEH-hahs deh mah-DEH-rah
work	obra	OH-brah
	trabajo	trah-BAH-hoh
work, completion of	terminación de obra	tehr-me-nah-seeON deh OH-brah

TOOLS
HERRAMIENTAS
eh-rrrah-meEHN-tahs

axe	hacha	*AH-chah*
ball-peen hammer	martillo de bola	*mahr-TEE-yoh deh BOH-lah*
bar	barreta	*bah-RRREH-tah*
blower	sopladora	*soh-plah-DOH-rah*
broom	escoba	*ehs-KOH-bah*
brush	pincel, brocheta	*PEEN-sehl, broh-CHEH-tah*
bucket	cubo	*KOO-boh*
carpenter's apron	mandil	*mahn-DEEL*
carpenter's square	escuadra	*ehs-KWAH-drah*
c-clamp	prensa de "C"	*PREHN-sah deh SEH*
chain pipe wrench	llave de cadena	*YAH-veh de kah-DEH-nah*
chain saw	sierra de cadena	*seeEH-rrrah deh kah-DEH-nah*
chisel wood	formón, cincel	*fohr-MOHN, SEEN-sehl*
circular saw	sierra circular (de mano)	*seeEH-rrrah seer-koo-LAHR (deh MAH-noh)*
claw hammer	martillo chivo	*mahr-TEE-yoh CHEE-voh*
combination square	escuadra de combinación	*ehs-KWAH-drah deh kohm-bee-nah-seeON*
compound mitre saw	sierra de corte angular	*seeEH-rrrah deh KOHR-teh ahn-goo-LAHR*
cut-off saw	sierra para cortar	*seeEH-rrrah PAH-rah kohr-TAHR*
drill	taladro	*tah-LAH-droh*
drill bit	barrena	*bah-RRREH-nah*
	taladro	*tah-LAH-droh*
drill (electric)	taladradora	*tah-lah-drah-DOH-rah*
file	lima	*LEE-mah*
flashlight	linterna	*leen-TEHR-nah*
flat head screwdriver	desarmador de hoja plana	*deh-sahr-mah-DOOR deh OH-hah PLAH-nah*
forklift	montacargas	*mohn-tah-CAR-gahs*
framing square	escuadra	*ehs-KWAH-drah*
funnel	embudo	*ehm-BOO-doh*
gloves	guantes	*GWAHN-tehs*
goggles	lentes de seguridad	*LEHN-tehs deh seh-goo-ree-DAHD*
hammer	martillo	*mahr-TEE-yoh*
hand saw	serrucho	*seh-RRROO-choh*

hoe	azadón	*ah-sah-DOHN*
hose	manguera	*mahn-GEH-rah*
jigsaw	sierra de vaivén	*seeEH-rrrah deh vah-ee-VEHN*
jointer	cepillo automático	*seh-PEE-yoh ah-oo-toh-MAH-tee-koh*
jointer plane	cepillo de mano	*seh-PEE-yoh deh MAH-noh*
knife (utility)	navaja	*nah-VAH-hah*
ladder	escalera	*ehs-kah-LEH-rah*
	(de mano)	*(deh MAH-noh)*
lawnmower	cortacésped	*kohr-tah-SEHS-pehd*
level	nivel	*nee-VEHL*
mallet	mazo	*MAH-soh*
mitre box	caja de corte	*KAH-hah deh KOHR-teh*
	angular	*ahn-goo-LAHR*
mitre saw	sierra de retroceso	*seeEH-rrrah deh reh-troh-SEH-soh*
	para ingletes	*PAH-rah een-GLEH-tehs*
mixer	mezcladora	*mehs-klah-DOH-rah*
	revolvedora	*reh-vohl-veh-DOH-rah*
nail gun	clavadora	*klah-vah-DOH-rah*
	automática	*ah-oo-toh-MAH-tee-kah*
phillips screwdriver	desarmador de	*dehs-ahr-mah-DOOR deh*
	punta en cruz	*POON-tah ehn kroos*
pick	pico	*PEE-koh*
pick-axe	zapapico	*sah-PAH-pee-koh*
plane	cepillo	*seh-PEE-yoh*
pliers	alicates	*ah-lee-KAH-tehs*
	pinzas	*PEEN-sahs*
plumb bob	plomada	*ploh-MAH-dah*
plumb line	hilo de plomada	*EE-loh deh ploh-MAH-dah*
pump	bomba	*BOHM-bah*
punches	punzones	*poon-SOH-nehs*
radial Saw	sierra fija	*seeEH-rrrah FEE-hah*
rake	rastrillo	*rahs-TREE-yoh*
rebar bender	doblador de	*doh-blah-DOOR deh*
	varilla	*vah-REE-yah*
reciprocating saw	sierra alternativa	seeEh-rrrah ahl-tehr-nah-tee-VAH
roller	aplanadora	*ah-plah-nah-DOH-rah*
	rodillo	*roh-DEE-yoh*
router	fresadora	*freh-sah-DOH-rah*
safety glasses	gafas de	*GAH-fahs deh*
	seguridad	*seh-goo-ree-DAHD*

sander	lijadora	*lee-hah-DOH-rah*
saw	sierra	*seeEH-rrrah*
saw (electric)	sierra eléctrica	*seeEH-rrrah eh-LEHK-tree-kah*
saw (hand)	serrucho	*seh-RRROO-choh*
sawhorse	burro	*BOO-rrroh*
screwdriver	destornillador	*dehs-tohr-nee-yah-DOOR*
	desarmador	*dehs-ahr-mah-DOOR*
sheet metal shears	tijeras para metal	*tee-HEH-rahs PAH-rah meh-TAHL*
shovel	pala	*PAH-lah*
sledgehammer	marro, mazo	*MAH-rrroh, MAH-soh*
square	escuadra	*ehs-KWAH-drah*
soldering torch	soplete	*soh-PLEH-teh*
stapler	engrapadora	*ehn-grah-pah-DOH-rah*
staple gun	engrapadora	*ehn-grah-pah-DOH-rah*
	automática	*ah-oo-toh-MAH-tee-kah*
table saw	sierra fija	*seeEH-rrrah FEE-hah*
	sierra de mesa	*seeEH-rrrah deh MEH-sah*
thread	hilo	*EE-loh*
tool box	caja de	*KAH-hah deh*
	herramientas	*eh-rrrah-meEHN-tahs*
t-square	regla "T"	*REH-glah teh*
wheel barrow	carretilla	*kah-rrreh-TEE-yah*
wrench	llave	*YAH-veh*
wrench (adjustable)	llave francesa	*YAH-veh frahn-SEH-sah*
wrench (plumbers)	llave inglesa	*YAH-veh een-GLEH-sah*
	perico	*peh-REE-koh*
work light	lámpara de	*LAHM-pah-rah deh*
	trabajo	*trah-BAH-hoh*

Tools

THE MONTHS OF THE YEAR
LOS MESES DEL AÑO
lohs MEH-sehs dehl AH-neeoh

January	enero	*eh-NEH-roh*
February	febrero	*feh-BREH-roh*
March	marzo	*MAHR-soh*
April	abril	*ah-BREEL*
May	mayo	*MAH-yoh*
June	junio	*HOO-neeoh*
July	julio	*HOO-leeoh*
August	agosto	*ah-GOHS-toh*
September	septiembre	*sep-teeEHM-breh*
October	octubre	*ohk-TO-breh*
November	noviembre	*noh-veeEHM-breh*
December	diciembre	*dee-seeEHM-breh*

THE DAYS OF THE WEEK
LOS DÍAS DE LA SEMANA
lohs DEE-ahs deh lah seh-MAH-nah

Monday	lunes	*LOO-nehs*
Tuesday	martes	*MAHR-tehs*
Wednesday	miércoles	*meEHR-koh-less*
Thursday	jueves	*hooEH-vehs*
Friday	viernes	*veeEHR-nehs*
Saturday	sábado	*SAH-bah-doh*
Sunday	domingo	*doh-MEEN-goh*

Months, Days, Numbers

NUMBERS
LOS NÚMEROS
lohs NOO-meh-rohs

0	cero	*SEH-roh*
1	uno	*OO-noh*
2	dos	*dohs*
3	tres	*trehs*
4	cuatro	*KWAH-troh*
5	cinco	*SEEN-koh*
6	seis	*SEH-ees*
7	sieta	*seeEH-teh*
8	ocho	*OH-choh*
9	nueve	*nooEH-veh*
10	diez	*dee-EHS*
11	once	*OHN-seh*
12	doce	*DOH-seh*
13	trece	*TREH-seh*
14	catorce	*kah-TOHR-seh*
15	quince	*KEEN-seh*
16	dieciseis	*dee-eh-see-SEH-ees*
17	diecisiete	*dee-eh-see-seeEH-teh*
18	dieciocho	*dee-eh-see-OH-choh*
19	diecinueve	*dee-eh-see-nooEH-veh*
20	viente	*VEIN-teh*
21	vientiuno	*vein-tee-OO-noh*
22	vientidos	*vein-tee-DOHS*
30	treinta	*TREH-in-tah*
31	treintiuno	*TREH-in-tah ee OOH-noh*
32	treintidos	*TREH-in-tah ee DOHS*
40	cuarenta	*kwah-REHN-tah*
50	cincuenta	*seen-KWEHN-tah*
60	sesenta	*seh-SEHN-tah*
70	setenta	*seh-TEHN-tah*
80	ochenta	*oh-CHEN-tah*
90	noventa	*noh-VEHN-tah*
100	cien	*see-EHN*
200	doscientos	*doh-see-EHN-tohs*
300	trescientos	*treh-see-EHN-tohs*
500	quinientos	*kee-nee-EHN-tohs*
1000	mil	*meel*

BASIC JOB QUESTIONS, ANSWERS AND STATEMENTS
Preguntas, respuestas y afirmaciones básicas en el trabajo
preh-GOON-tahs, rehs-pooh-ehs-TAHS ee ah-feer-mah-seeOH-nehs BAH-see-kahs ehn ehl trah-BAH-hoh

How many men do you have to help you?
¿Cuántos hombres tiene para ayudarlo/a?
KWAHN-tohs OHM-brehs teeEH-neh PAH-rah ah-YOU-dahr-loh/lah?

I have _____ men to help me.
Tengo _____ hombres para ayudarme.
TEHN-goh _____ OHM-brehs PAH-rah ah-YOU-dahr-meh.

How big is your crew?
¿Cuán grande es su cuadrilla/equipo?
kwahn GRAHN-deh ehs soo KWAH-dree-yah/eh-KEY-poh?

My crew has ___ men.
Mi cuadrilla/equipo tiene _____ hombres.
me KWAH-dree-yah/eh-KEY-poh teeEH-neh _____ OHM-brehs.

Do you have your own tools?
¿Tiene sus propias herramientas?
teeEH-neh soos PROH-peeahs eh-rrrah-meEHN-tahs?

When can you start the job?
¿Cuándo puede comenzar con este trabajo?
KWAHN-doh pooh-EH-deh koh-mehn-SAHR kohn EHS-teh trah-BAH-hoh?

I can begin the job next week.
Puedo comenzar con este trabajo la semana que viene.
pooh-EH-doh koh-mehn-SAHR kohn EHS-teh trah-BAH-hoh lah seh-MAH-nah keh vee-EH-neh.

How long will it take you to do the job?
¿Cuánto le tomará completar el trabajo?
KWAHN-toh leh toh-mah-RAH kohm-pleh-TAHR ehl trah-BAH-hoh?

It will take a month/week/day to do the job.
Tomará un mes/una semana/un día terminar el trabajo.
toh-mah-RAH oon mehs/OO-nah seh-MAH-nah/oon DEE-ah tehr-me-NAHR ehl trah-BAH-hoh.

Can you give me a bid to do another job?
¿Puede darme un estimado para hacer otro trabajo?
pooh-EH-deh DAHR-meh oon ehs-tee-MAH-doh PAH-rah ah-SEHR OH-troh trah-BAH-hoh?

We can give you a bid to do another job.
Podemos darle un estimado para hacer otro trabajo.
poh-DEH-mohs DAHR-leh oon ehs-tee-MAH-doh PAH-rah ah-SEHR OH-troh trah-BAH-hoh.

Can you work tomorrow?
¿Puede trabajar mañana?
pooh-EH-deh trah-bah-HAHR mah-nee-AH-nah?

I can work everyday.
Puedo trabajar todos los días.
pooh-EH-doh trah-bah-HAHR TOH-dohs lohs DEE-ahs.

How much does this job pay?
¿Cuánto paga este trabajo?
KWAHN-toh PAH-gah EHS-teh trah-BAH-hoh?

Your pay is going to be $_____ per hour.
Su paga será _____ dólares la hora.
soo PAH-gah seh-RAH _____ DOH-lah-rehs lah OH-rah.

When is pay day?
¿Cuándo es el día de pago?
KWAHN-doh ehs ehl DEE-ah deh PAH-goh?

I will pay you at the end of the week/day/job.
Le pagaré al final de la semana/del día/del trabajo.
leh pah-GAH-reh ahl fee-NAHL deh lah seh-MAH-nah/dehl DEE-ah/dehl trah-BAH-hoh.

CONVERSATIONAL
En conversación
ehn kohn-vehr-sah-seeON

How are you today?
¿Cómo está usted hoy/Cómo le va?
KOH-moh ehs-TAH oos-TEHD ohEE/KOH-moh leh vah?

How is your family?
¿Cómo está su familia?
KOH-moh ehs-TAH soo fah-ME-leeah?

Very well, thank you.
Muy bien, gracias.
mooEE bee-EHN, GRAH-seeahs.

I will see you tomorrow.
Nos vemos mañana.
nohs VEH-mohs mah-nee-AH-nah

I will not be here tomorrow.
No estaré aquí mañana.
noh ehs-tah-REH ah-KEY mah-nee-AH-nah.

Did you have a good weekend?
¿Pasó un buen fin de semana?
pah-SOH oon bwehn feen deh seh-MAH-nah?

Yes, I had a very good weekend.
Sí, pasé un muy buen fin de semana.
see, pah-SEH oon mooEE bwehn feen deh seh-MAH-nah.

You have a good crew of men.
Tiene un buen equipo de hombres.
teeEH-neh oon bwehn eh-KEY-poh deh OHM-brehs.

Do you want to take a lunch break?
¿Quiere tomar un descanso para almorzar?
keeEH-reh toh-MAHR oon dehs-KAHN-soh PAH-rah ahl-more-SAHR?

Your work looks good.
Su trabajo se ve bien.
soo trah-BAH-hoh seh veh beEHN.

I am going to the store, do you need anything?
¿Voy a la tienda, necesita algo?
vohEE ah lah tee-EHN-dah, neh-seh-SEE-tah AHL-goh?

What time is it?
¿Qué hora es?
keh oh-RAH ehs?

GENERAL
General
heh-neh-RAHL

Do you speak English?
¿Habla inglés?
AH-blah een-GLEHS?

Do you speak Spanish?
¿Habla español?
AH-blah ehs-pah-nee-OHL?

Yes.
Sí.
see.

No.
No.
noh.

Please.
Por favor.
pore fah-VOHR.

Thank you.
Gracias.
GRAH-seeahs.

What is your name?
¿Cuál es su nombre/Cómo se llama?
kwAHL ehs soo NOHM-breh/KOH-moh seh YAH-mah?

My name is…../Me llamo…
Mi nombre es…/Me llamo…
me NOHM-breh ehs…/meh YAH-moh…

Do you have references?
¿Tiene referencias?
teeEH-neh reh-feh-REHN-seeahs?

Yes, I have references.
Sí, tengo referencias.
see, TEHN-goh reh-feh-REHN-seeahs.

No, I do not have references.
No, no tengo referencias.
noh, noh TEHN-goh reh-feh-REHN-seeahs.

What is your phone number?
¿Cuál es su número de teléfono?
kwAHL ehs soo NOO-meh-roh deh teh-LEH-foh-noh?

My phone number is_____.
Mi número es _____.
me NOO-meh-roh ehs _____.

MISCELLANEOUS
Misceláneos
me-seh-LAH-nehohs

Drug use is not tolerated.
No se permite el uso de drogas.
noh seh pehr-ME-teh ehl OO-soh deh-SAHR DROH-gahs.

Do you have a driver's license?
¿Tiene licencia de conducir?
teeEH-neh lee-SEHN-see-ah deh kohn-do-SEER?

Where can I get a driver's license?
¿Adónde puedo conseguir una licencia de conducir?
ah-DON-deh pooh-EH-doh kohn-seh-GEER OO-nah lee-SEHN-see-ah deh kohn-do-SEER?

Where is the hospital/clinic?
¿Adónde hay un hospital/una clínica?
ah-DON-deh AHee oon ohs-pee-TAHL/OO-nah KLEE-nee-kah?

Hold it there while I nail it.
Sosténgalo allí mientras lo clavo.
sohs-TEHN-gah-loh ah-YEE meEHN-trahs loh KLAH-voh.

Pick this up.
Recoja esto.
reh-KOH-hah EHS-toh.

Raise it a little.
Levántelo un poco.
leh-VAHN-teh-loh oon POH-koh.

Lower it a little
Bájelo un poco.
BAH-heh-loh oon POH-koh.

Hammer this.
Martille esto.
mahr-TEE-yeh EHS-toh.

Get someone to help you.
Consiga a alguien que lo ayude.
kohn-SEE-gah ah AHL-gee-ehn keh loh ah-YOO-deh.

Where…Where is…. Where are…. What is that?
¿Adónde…Adónde está…Adónde están…Qué es eso?
ah-DON-deh… ah-DON-deh ehs-TAH…ah-DON-deh ehs-TAHN…keh ehs EH-soh?

Be careful!
¡Tenga cuidado!
TEHN-gah kwee-DAH-doh!

Phrases

Follow me.
Sígame.
SEE-gah-meh.

Push.
Empuje.
ehm-POOH-heh.

Pull.
Jale.
HAH-leh.

Watch out!
¡Cuidado!
kwee-DAH-doh!

Help me carry this.
Ayúdeme a cargar esto.
ah-YOU-deh-meh ah kahr-GAHR EHS-toh.

Let me help you with that.
Déjeme ayudarle con eso.
DEH-heh-meh ah-you-DAHR-leh kohn EH-soh.

The key will be hidden here.
La llave estará escondida aquí.
lah YAH-veh ehs-tah-RAH ehs-kohn-DEE-dah ah-KEY.

Please lock the door when you leave.
Por favor cierre la puerta con llave antes de irse.
pore fah-VOHR see-EH-rrreh lah pooh-EHR-tah kohn YAH-veh AHN-tehs deh EER-seh.

The port-a-pot is out back.
El baño portable está allí atrás.
ehl BAH-neeoh pore-TAH-bleh ehs-TAH ah-YEE ah-TRAHS.

The dumpster is over there.
El basurero está allá.
ehl bah-soo-REH-roh ehs-TAH ah-YAH.

Phrases

CONCRETE
Concreto
kohn-KREH-toh

How long have you been working with concrete?
¿Cuánto hace que trabaja con concreto?
KWAHN-toh AH-seh keh trah-BAH-hah kohn kohn-KREH-toh?

I have been working with concrete for ___ years.
Hace _____ años que trabajo con concreto.
AH-seh _____ AH-neeohs keh trah-BAH-hoh kohn kohn-KREH-toh.

Do you have references?
¿Tiene referencias?
teeEH-neh reh-feh-REHN-seeahs?

Yes, I have references.
Sí, tengo referencias.
see, TEHN-goh reh-feh-REHN-seeahs.

No, I do not have references.
No, no tengo referencias.
noh, noh TEHN-goh reh-feh-REHN-seeahs.

Can you give me an estimate for this job?
¿Me puede dar un presupuesto por este trabajo?
meh pooh-EH-deh dahr oon preh-soo-pooEHS-toh pore EHS-teh trah-BAH-hoh?

When can you start this project?
¿Cuándo puede comenzar con este proyecto?
KWAHN-doh pooh-EH-deh koh-mehn-SAHR kohn EHS-teh proh-YEHK-toh?

I can start this job next week/in two weeks.
Puedo comenzar este trabajo la semana que viene/en dos semanas.
pooh-EH-doh koh-mehn-SAHR EHS-teh trah-BAH-hoh lah seh-MAH-nah keh vee-EH-neh/ehn DOHS seh-MAH-nahs.

How long will it take you to complete this job?
¿Cuánto le tomará completar este trabajo?
KWAHN-toh leh toh-mah-RAH kohm-pleh-TAHR EHS-teh trah-BAH-hoh?

It will take a day/week to finish.
Tomará un día/una semana terminarlo.
toh-mah-RAH oon DEE-ah/OO-nah seh-MAH-nah tehr-me-NAHR-loh.

Do you have your own tools?
¿Tiene sus propias herramientas?
teeEH-neh soos PROH-peeahs eh-rrrah-meEHN-tahs?

Phrases

Is it going to rain?
¿Lloverá?
yoh-veh-RAH?

We need to build forms here.
Debemos construir encofrados aquí.
deh-BEH-mohs kohns-troo-EER ehn-koh-FRAH-dohs ah-KEY.

We will pour the concrete tomorrow.
Vaciaremos el concreto mañana.
Vah-see-ah-REH-mohs ehl kohn-KREH-toh mah-nee-AH-nah.

We need to smooth-out that spot in the concrete.
Debemos alisar ese punto en el concreto.
deh-BEH-mohs ah-lee-SAHR EH-seh poon-TOH ehn ehl kohn-KREH-toh.

We need to make this a smooth finish.
Debemos darle a esto una terminación lisa.
deh-BEH-mohs DAHR-leh ah EHS-toh OO-nah tehr-me-nah-seeON LEE-sah.

We need a straight edge.
Necesitamos un borde recto.
neh-seh-see-TAH-mohs oon BOHR-deh REHK-toh.

We need to power wash the concrete.
Debemos lavar el concreto a presión.
deh-BEH-mohs lah-VAHR ehl kohn-KREH-toh ah preh-seeON.

We need to tamp this area down.
Debemos apisonar este área.
deh-BEH-mohs ah-pee-soh-NAHR EHS-teh AH-reh-ah.

We need a level.
Necesitamos un nivel.
neh-seh-see-TAH-mohs oon NEE-vehl.

We need to laser level.
Debemos nivelar con el nivel láser.
deh-BEH-mohs nee-veh-LAHR kohn ehl nee-VEHL LAH-sehr.

We need to cover the concrete with plastic.
Debemos cubrir el concreto con plástico.
deh-BEH-mohs koo-BREER ehl kohn-KREH-toh kohn PLAHS-tee-koh.

We need more bags of concrete.
Necesitamos más bolsas de concreto.
neh-seh-see-TAH-mohs mahs BOHL-sahs deh kohn-KREH-toh.

We need more stakes.
Necesitamos más estacas.
neh-seh-see-TAH-mohs mahs ehs-TAH-kahs.

We need more lumber.
Necesitamos más madera.
neh-seh-see-TAH-mohs mahs mah-DEH-rah.

We need more plywood.
Necesitamos más tableros de madera.
neh-seh-see-TAH-mohs mahs tah-BLEH-rohs deh mah-DEH-rah.

We need more wire mesh.
Necesitamos más tela metálica.
neh-seh-see-TAH-mohs mahs TEH-lah meh-TAH-lee-kah.

We need more rebar.
Necesitamos más barras de refuerzo.
neh-seh-see-TAH-mohs mahs BAH-rrrahs deh reh-FWEHR-soh.

We need more rebar saddles and anchoring wire.
Necesitamos más barras de refuerzo y más alambre de anclaje.
neh-seh-see-TAH-mohs mahs BAH-rrrahs deh reh-FWEHR-soh ee mahs ah-LAHM-breh deh ahn-KLAH-heh.

Where is the rake?
¿Adónde está el rastrillo?
ah-DON-deh ehs-TAH ehl rahs-TREE-yoh?

Where is the shovel?
¿Adónde está la pala?
ah-DON-deh ehs-TAH lah PAH-lah?

Where is the bull-float?
¿Adónde está el aplanador?
ah-DON-deh ehs-TAH ehl ah-plah-nah-DOOR?

Where is the metal mesh?
¿Adónde está la tela metálica?
ah-DON-deh ehs-TAH lah TEH-lah meh-TAH-lee-kah?

Where is the rebar?
¿Adónde está la barra de refuerzo?
ah-DON-deh ehs-TAH lah BAH-rrrah deh reh-FWEHR-soh?

Where is the caution tape?
¿Adónde está la cinta de precaución?
ah-DON-deh ehs-TAH lah SEEN-tah deh preh-kahw-seeON?

Where is the bench mark?
¿Adónde está la cota/el punto de referencia?
ah-DON-deh ehs-TAH lah KOH-tah/ehl POON-toh deh reh-feh-REHN-seeah?

How many yards of concrete will be needed?
¿Cuántas yardas de concreto se van a necesitar?
KWAHN-tahs YAHR-dahs deh kohn-KREH-toh seh vahn ah neh-seh-SEE-tahr?

We need the fiberglass reinforced concrete.
Necesitamos el concreto que está reforzado con fibra de vidrio.
neh-seh-see-TAH-mohs ehl kohn-KREH-toh keh ehs-TAH reh-fohr-SAH-doh kohn fee-BRAH deh VEE-dreeoh.

The concrete needs to be 3,000 psi/5,000 psi.
El concreto debe ser de 3.000 libras por pulgada cuadrada/5.000 libras por pulgada cuadrada.
ehl kohn-KREH-toh DEH-beh sehr deh trehs-MEEL LEE-bras pore pool-GAH-dah kwah-DRAH-dah/SEEN-koh-MEEL LEE-bras pore pool-GAH-dah kwah-DRAH-dah.

The truck will deliver ____ yards of concrete tomorrow.
El camión entregará _____ yardas de concreto mañana.
ehl kah-meON ehn-treh-gah-RAH _____ YAHR-dahs deh kohn-KREH-toh mah-nee-AH-nah.

Notify me when the truck arrives.
Avíseme cuando llegue el camión.
ah-VEE-seh-meh KWAHN-doh YEH-geh ehl kah-meON.

We need to get the footings inspected before we pour the concrete.
Debemos inspeccionar el cimiento antes de volcar el concreto.
deh-BEH-mohs eens-pek-seeoh-NAHR ehl see-meEHN-toh AHN-tehs deh vohl-KAHR ehl kohn-KREH-toh.

We need to clean up the job-site daily.
Debemos limpiar el área de trabajo a diario.
deh-BEH-mohs leem-peeAHR ehl AH-reh-ah deh trah-BAH-hoh ah dee-AH-reeoh.

DEMOLITION/CLEAN-UP
Demolición/Limpieza de obra
deh-moh-lee-seeON/leem-peeEH-sah deh OH-brah

Have you ever done tear-out/demolition work before?
¿Ha realizado anteriormemente trabajo de remoción/demolición?
ah rreh-ah-lee-SAH-doh ahn-teh-ree-ohr-MEHN-teh trah-BAH-hoh deh reh-moh-seeON/deh-moh-LEE-seeON?

I have been doing tear out/demolition work for _____ years.

Hace _____ años que realizo trabajo de remoción/demolición.

AH-seh _____ AH-neeohs keh reh-ah-LEE-soh trah-BAH-hoh deh reh-moh-seeON/deh-moh-lee-seeON.

Do you have references?

¿Tiene referencias?

teeEH-neh reh-feh-REHN-seeahs?

Yes, I have references.

Sí, tengo referencias.

see, TEHN-goh reh-feh-REHN-seeahs.

No, I do not have references.

No, no tengo referencias.

noh, noh TEHN-goh reh-feh-REHN-seeahs.

Can you give me an estimate for this job?

¿Me puede dar un presupuesto por este trabajo?

meh pooh-EH-deh dahr oon preh-soo-pooEHS-toh pore EHS-teh trah-BAH-hoh?

When can you start this project?

¿Cuándo puede comenzar con este proyecto?

KWAHN-doh pooh-EH-deh koh-mehn-SAHR kohn EHS-teh proh-YEHK-toh?

I can start this job next week/in two weeks.

Puedo comenzar este trabajo la semana que viene/en dos semanas.

pooh-EH-doh koh-mehn-SAHR EHS-teh trah-BAH-hoh lah seh-MAH-nah keh vee-EH-neh/ehn DOHS seh-MAH-nahs.

How long will it take you to complete this job?

¿Cuánto le tomará completar este trabajo?

KWAHN-toh leh toh-mah-RAH kohm-pleh-TAHR EHS-teh trah-BAH-hoh?

It will take a day/week to finish.

Tomará un día/una semana terminarlo.

toh-mah-RAH oon DEE-ah/OO-nah seh-MAH-nah tehr-me-NAHR-loh.

Do you have your own tools?

¿Tiene sus propias herramientas?

teeEH-neh soos PROH-peeahs eh-rrrah-meEHN-tahs?

We need to tear-out all the walls and ceilings marked with orange paint.

Debemos demoler todas las paredes y cielorrasos marcados con pintura anaranjada.

deh-BEH-mohs deh-moh-LEHR TOH-dahs lahs pah-REH-dehs ee see-eh-loh-RRRAH-sohs mahr-KAH-dohs kohn peen-TO-rah ah-nah-rahn-HAH-dah.

We need to stack the bricks up after we get the old cement off of them.
Debemos apilar los ladrillos luego de retirarles el cemento viejo.
deh-BEH-mohs ah-pee-LAHR lohs lah-DREE-yohs loo-EH-goh deh reh-tee-RAHR-lehs ehl seh-MEHN-toh vee-EH-hoh.

We need to put all the rocks in one pile.
Debemos apilar todas las rocas.
deh-BEH-mohs ah-pee-LAHR TOH-dahs lahs ROH-kahs.

We need to stack all the debris in the dumpster neatly.
Debemos apilar todos los escombros prolijamente en el basurero.
deh-BEH-mohs ah-pee-LAHR TOH-dohs lohs ehs-KOHM-brohs proh-lee-hah-MEHN-teh ehn ehl bah-soo-REH-roh.

Is the dumpster full yet?
¿Ya está lleno el basurero?
yah ehs-TAH YEH-noh ehl bah-soo-REH-roh?

Let me know when the dumpster is almost full.
Avíseme cuando el basurero esté casi lleno.
ah-VEE-seh-meh KWAHN-doh ehl bah-soo-REH-roh ehs-TEH KAH-see YEH-noh.

We need to clean up the yard.
Debemos limpiar el jardín.
deh-BEH-mohs leem-peeAHR ehl hahr-DEEN.

We need to rake the yard.
Debemos rastrillar el jardín.
deh-BEH-mohs rahs-TREE-yahr ehl hahr-DEEN.

We need to sweep this up.
Debemos barrer esto.
deh-BEH-mohs bah-RRREHR EHS-toh.

Where is the hammer?
¿Adónde está el martillo?
ah-DON-deh ehs-TAH ehl mahr-TEE-yoh?

Where is the broom?
¿Adónde está la escoba?
ah-DON-deh ehs-TAH lah ehs-KOH-bah?

Where is the shovel?
¿Adónde está la pala?
ah-DON-deh ehs-TAH lah PAH-lah?

Phrases

Where is the sledgehammer?
¿Adónde está el marro/mazo?
ah-DON-deh ehs-TAH ehl MAH-rrroh/MAH-soh?

Where is the crow-bar?
¿Adónde está la pata de cabra/palanca?
ah-DON-deh ehs-TAH ehl lah PAH-tah deh KAH-brah pah-LAHN-kah?

Where is the wheel-barrow?
¿Adónde está la carretilla?
ah-DON-deh ehs-TAH lah kah-rrreh-TEE-yah?

Where are the gloves?
¿Adónde están los guantes?
ah-DON-deh ehs-TAHN lohs GWAHN-tehs?

Where are the safety goggles?
¿Adónde están los lentes de seguridad?
ah-DON-deh ehs-TAHN lohs LEHN-tehs deh seh-goo-ree-DAHD?

We need to sweep the floors.
Debemos barrer los pisos.
deh-BEH-mohs bah-RRREHR lohs PEE-sohs.

We need another dumpster.
Necesitamos otro basurero.
neh-seh-see-TAH-mohs OH-troh bah-soo-REH-roh.

We need more gloves.
Necesitamos más guantes.
neh-seh-see-TAH-mohs mahs GWAHN-tehs.

We need to jack-hammer this concrete out.
Debemos taladrar este concreto.
deh-BEH-mohs tah-LAH-drahr ehs-TEH kohn-KREH-toh.

We need to use the back hoe to fix this yard.
Debemos utilizar la retroexcavadora para arreglar este jardín.
deh-BEH-mohs oo-tee-lee-SAHR lah reh-troh-ex-kah-vah-DOH-rah PAH-rah ah-rrreh-GLAHR EHS-teh hahr-DEEN.

We need to remove this.
Debemos remover esto.
deh-BEH-mohs reh-moh-VEHR EHS-toh.

We need to leave this.
Debemos dejar esto.
deh-BEH-mohs deh-HAHR EHS-toh.

We need to tear this out.
Debemos demoler esto.
deh-BEH-mohs deh-moh-LEHR EHS-toh.

We need to remove the old bricks.
Debemos remover los ladrillos viejos.
deh-BEH-mohs reh-moh-VEHR lohs lah-DREE-yohs vee-EH-hohs.

We need to remove the old siding.
Debemos remover el revestimiento viejo.
deh-BEH-mohs reh-moh-VEHR ehl reh-vehs-tee-meEHN-toh vee-EH-hoh.

We need to remove this wood.
Debemos remover esta madera.
deh-BEH-mohs reh-moh-VEHR ehs-TAH mah-DEH-rah.

We need ___ men for this job.
Necesitamos _____ hombres para este trabajo.
neh-seh-see-TAH-mohs _____ OHM-brehs PAH-rah EHS-teh trah-BAH-hoh.

The port-a-pot is out back.
El baño portable está allí atrás.
ehl BAH-neeoh pore-TAH-bleh ehs-TAH ah-YEE ah-TRAHS.

We need to clean up the job-site daily.
Debemos limpiar el área de trabajo a diario.
deh-BEH-mohs leem-peeAHR ehl AH-reh-ah deh trah-BAH-hoh ah dee-AH-reeoh.

DRY WALL
Muro en seco
MOO-roh ehn SEH-koh

How long have you been hanging dry wall?
¿Cuánto hace que trabaja colocando muros en seco?
KWAHN-toh AH-seh keh trah-BAH-hah koh-loh-CAN-doh MOO-rohs ehn SEH-koh?

How long have you been finishing dry wall?
¿Cuánto hace que trabaja en la terminación de muros en seco?
KWAHN-toh AH-seh keh trah-BAH-hah ehn lah tehr-me-nah-seeON deh MOO-rohs ehn SEH-koh?

I have been working with dry wall for ___ years.
Hace _____ años que trabajo con muros en seco.
AH-seh _____ AH-neeohs keh trah-BAH-hoh kohn MOO-rohs ehn SEH-koh.

Phrases

Do you have references?
¿Tiene referencias?
teeEH-neh reh-feh-REHN-seeahs?

Yes, I have references.
Sí, tengo referencias.
see, TEHN-goh reh-feh-REHN-seeahs.

No, I do not have references.
No, no tengo referencias.
noh, noh TEHN-goh reh-feh-REHN-seeahs.

Can you give me an estimate for this job?
¿Me puede dar un presupuesto por este trabajo?
meh pooh-EH-deh dahr oon preh-soo-pooEHS-toh pore EHS-teh trah-BAH-hoh?

When can you start this project?
¿Cuándo puede comenzar con este proyecto?
KWAHN-doh pooh-EH-deh koh-mehn-SAHR kohn EHS-teh proh-YEHK-toh?

I can start this job next week/in two weeks.
Puedo comenzar este trabajo la semana que viene/en dos semanas.
pooh-EH-doh koh-mehn-SAHR EHS-teh trah-BAH-hoh lah seh-MAH-nah keh vee-EH-neh/ehn DOHS seh-MAH-nahs.

How long will it take you to complete this job?
¿Cuánto le tomará completar este trabajo?
KWAHN-toh leh toh-mah-RAH kohm-pleh-TAHR EHS-teh trah-BAH-hoh?

It will take a day/week to finish.
Tomará un día/una semana terminarlo.
toh-mah-RAH oon DEE-ah/OO-nah seh-MAH-nah tehr-me-NAHR-loh.

Do you have your own tools?
¿Tiene sus propias herramientas?
teeEH-neh soos PROH-peeahs eh-rrrah-meeEHN-tahs?

We need more boards.
Necesitamos más tablas.
neh-seh-see-TAH-mohs mahs TAH-blahs.

We need more mud.
Necesitamos más barro.
neh-seh-see-TAH-mohs mahs BAH-rrroh.

We need more tape.
Necesitamos más cinta.
neh-seh-see-TAH-mohs mahs SEEN-tah.

We need more corner bead.
Necesitamos más esquineros.
neh-seh-see-TAH-mohs mahs ehs-key-NEH-rohs.

We need to finish this to a smooth finish.
Debemos darle a esto una terminación lisa.
deh-BEH-mohs DAHR-leh a EHS-toh OO-nah tehr-me-nah-seeON LEE-sah.

How many boards will you need?
¿Cuántas tablas va a necesitar?
KWAHN-tahs TAH-blahs vah a neh-seh-SEE-tahr?

Where is the mud?
¿Adónde está el barro?
ah-DON-deh ehs-TAH ehl BAH-rrroh?

Where is the tape?
¿Adónde está la cinta?
ah-DON-deh ehs-TAH lah SEEN-tah?

Where are the finishing tools?
¿Adónde están las herramientas de terminación?
ah-DON-deh ehs-TAHN lahs eh-rrrah-meEHN-tahs deh tehr-me-nah-seeON?

We need to use mesh tape here.
Debemos utilizar cinta de tela aquí.
deh-BEH-mohs oo-tee-lee-SAHR SEEN-tah deh TEH-lah ah-KEY.

We need to put the fan in here.
Debemos colocar el ventilador aquí.
deh-BEH-mohs koh-loh-CAR ehl vehn-tee-lah-DOOR ah-KEY.

We need more scaffolding.
Necesitamos más andamiaje.
neh-seh-see-TAH-mohs mahs ahn-dah-meAH-heh.

When will the boards be delivered?
¿Cuándo entregarán las tablas?
KWAHN-doh ehn-treh-gah-RAHN lahs TAH-blahs?

We need to stack the boards there.
Debemos apilar las tablas allí.
deh-BEH-mohs ah-pee-LAHR lahs TAH-blahs ah-YEE.

We need to use 2″ screws/1″ screws.
Debemos utilizar tornillos de 2 y de 1 pulgadas.
deh-BEH-mohs oo-tee-lee-SAHR tohr-NEE-yohs deh dohs y deh OO-nah ee oon KWAHR-toh pool-GAH-dahs.

Phrases

We need to repair this plaster.
Debemos reparar este yeso.
deh-BEH-mohs reh-pah-RAHR EHS-teh YEH-soh.

We need to fix the cracks in the wall.
Debemos arreglar las rajas/grietas en la pared.
deh-BEH-mohs ah-rrreh-GLAHR lahs RAH-hahs/gree-EH-tahs ehn lah pah-REHD.

We need to use mesh tape for fixing cracks.
Debemos utilizar cinta de tela para arreglar las rajas/grietas.
deh-BEH-mohs oo-tee-lee-SAHR SEEN-tah deh TEH-lah PAH-rah ah-rrreh-GLAHR lahs RAH-hahs/gree-EH-tahs.

We need to use _____" / 5/8" dry wall.
Debemos utilizar muro en seco de _____ pulgada/de 5/8 de pulgada.
deh-BEH-mohs oo-tee-lee-SAHR MOO-roh ehn SEH-koh deh MEH-deeah pool-GAH-dah/deh SEEN-koh ohk-TAH-vohs deh pool-GAH-dah.

We need to hang the ceilings first.
Debemos colgar primero los cielorrasos.
deh-BEH-mohs kohl-GAHR pree-MEH-roh lohs see-eh-loh-RRRAH-sohs.

We need to use the 20 minute/45 minute mud.
Debemos utilizar el barro de 20 minutos/45 minutos.
deh-BEH-mohs oo-tee-lee-SAHR ehl BAH-rrroh deh VEIN-teh me-NOO-tohs/kwah-rehn-TAH ee SEEN-koh me-NOO-tohs.

How many corner beads will be needed?
¿Cuántos esquineros se necesitarán?
KWAHN-tohs ehs-key-NEH-rohs seh neh-seh-see-tah-RAHN?

We need to flat tape this area.
Debemos cubrir este área con cinta.
deh-BEH-mohs koo-BREER EHS-teh AH-reh-ah kohn SEEN-tah.

We need to use corner tape here.
Debemos colocar cinta esquinera aquí.
deh-BEH-mohs oo-tee-lee-SAHR SEEN-tah ehs-key-NEH-rah ah-KEY.

We need to put scrap dry wall in the dumpster.
Debemos colocar el muro en seco de desecho en el basurero.
deh-BEH-mohs koh-loh-CAR ehl MOO-roh ehn SEH-koh deh deh-SEH-choh ehn ehl bah-soo-REH-roh.

We need to sand this area more.
Debemos arenar más éste área.
deh-BEH-mohs ah-reh-NAHR mahs EHS-teh AH-reh-ah.

We need to skim this area one more time.
Debemos razar éste área una vez más.
deh-BEH-mohs rah-SAHR EHS-teh AH-reh-ah OO-nah vehs mahs.

We need to clean up the job-site daily.
Debemos limpiar el área de trabajo a diario.
deh-BEH-mohs leem-peeAHR ehl AH-reh-ah deh trah-BAH-hoh ah dee-AH-reeoh.

ELECTRICAL
Electricidad
eh-lek-tree-see-DAHD

How long have you been an electrician?
¿Cuánto hace que es electricista?
KWAHN-toh AH-seh keh ehs eh-lek-tree-SEES-tah?

I have been an electrician for ___ years.
Hace _____ años que soy electricista.
AH-seh _____ AH-neeohs keh sohEE eh-lek-tree-SEES-tah.

Do you have references?
¿Tiene referencias?
teeEH-neh reh-feh-REHN-seeahs?

Yes, I have references.
Sí, tengo referencias.
see, TEHN-goh reh-feh-REHN-seeahs.

No, I do not have references.
No, no tengo referencias.
noh, noh TEHN-goh reh-feh-REHN-seeahs.

Can you give me an estimate for this job?
¿Me puede dar un presupuesto por este trabajo?
meh pooh-EH-deh dahr oon preh-soo-pooEHS-toh pore EHS-teh trah-BAH-hoh?

When can you start this project?
¿Cuándo puede comenzar con este proyecto?
KWAHN-doh pooh-EH-deh koh-mehn-SAHR kohn EHS-teh proh-YEHK-toh?

I can start this job next week/in two weeks.
Puedo comenzar este trabajo la semana que viene/en dos semanas.
pooh-EH-doh koh-mehn-SAHR EHS-teh trah-BAH-hoh lah seh-MAH-nah keh vee-EH-neh/ehn DOHS seh-MAH-nahs.

How long will it take you to complete this job?
¿Cuánto le tomará completar este trabajo?
KWAHN-toh leh toh-mah-RAH kohm-pleh-TAHR EHS-teh trah-BAH-hoh?

Phrases

It will take a day/week to finish.
Tomará un día/una semana terminarlo.
toh-mah-RAH oon DEE-ah/OO-nah seh-MAH-nah tehr-me-NAHR-loh.

Do you have your own tools?
¿Tiene sus propias herramientas?
teeEH-neh soos PROH-peeahs eh-rrrah-meEHN-tahs?

We need to rough in the house.
Debemos hacer las conexiones de tubería y de electricidad a la casa.
deh-BEH-mohs ah-SEHR lahs koh-nehx-seeOH-nehs deh to-beh-REE-ah ee deh eh-lehk-tree-see-DAHD ah lah KAH-sah.

We need to install the light fixtures.
Debemos instalar los artefactos de iluminación.
deh-BEH-mohs eens-tah-LAHR lohs ahr-teh-FAK-tohs deh ee-loo-me-nah-seeON.

Phrases

We need to install can lights in this room.
Debemos instalar luces de tarro en esta habitación.
deh-BEH-mohs eens-tah-LAHR LOO-sehs deh TAH-rrroh ehn EHS-tah ah-bee-tah-seeON.

We need to wire the laundry room for 220 volts.
Debemos cablear el lavadero con electricidad de 220 voltios.
deh-BEH-mohs kah-blehAHR ehl lah-vah-DEH-roh kohn eh-lek-tree-see-DAHD deh dohs-seeEHN-tohs VOL-teeohs.

We need 110 volts here.
Necesitamos 110 voltios aquí.
neh-seh-see-TAH-mohs seeEHN-toh deeEHS VOL-teeohs ah-KEY.

We need 220 volts here.
Necesitamos 220 voltios aquí.
neh-seh-see-TAH-mohs dohs-seeEHN-tohs VEIN-teh VOL-teeohs ah-KEY.

We need to wire for under-cabinet lights in the kitchen.
Debemos cablear para luces de bajo mesada en la cocina.
deh-BEH-mohs kah-blehAHR PAH-rah LOO-sehs deh BAH-hoh meh-SAH-dah ehn lah koh-SEE-nah.

Are the fixtures in yet?
¿Llegaron ya los artefactos?
yeh-GAH-rohn yah lohs ahr-teh-FAHK-tohs?

We need to put this light in the bedroom/bathroom/kitchen.
Debemos colocar esta luz en el dormitorio/baño/la cocina.
deh-BEH-mohs koh-loh-CAR EHS-tah loose ehn ehl door-me-TOH-reeoh/BAH-neeoh/lah koh-SEE-nah.

We need to put this chandelier in the dining room/foyer.
Debemos colocar esta araña (de luces) en el comedor/vestíbulo.
deh-BEH-mohs koh-loh-CAR EHS-tah ah-RAH-neeah (deh LOO-sehs) ehn ehl koh-meh-DOOR/vehs-TEE-boo-loh.

How many plugs/switches are in that room?
¿Cuántos enchufes/interruptores hay en esa habitación?
¿KWAHN-tohs ehn-CHOO-fehs/een-teh-rrroop-TOH-rehs ahEE ehn EH-sah ah-bee-tah-seeON?

We need to put the face-plates on the plugs and switches.
Debemos colocarle las tapas a los enchufes y a los interruptores.
deh-BEH-mohs koh-loh-CAR-leh lahs TAH-pahs ah lohs ehn-CHOO-fehs ee ah lohs een-teh-rrroop-TOH-rehs.

We need to get the electricity turned on.
Debemos conectar/encender la electricidad.
deh-BEH-mohs koh-nek-TAHR/ehn-sehn-DEHR lah eh-lek-tree-see-DAHD.

We need to get the electricity turned off.
Debemos desconectar/apagar la electricidad.
deh-BEH-mohs dehs-koh-nek-TAHR/ah-pah-GAHR lah eh-lek-tree-see-DAHD.

We need to get the temporary pole installed.
Debemos instalar el poste temporario.
deh-BEH-mohs eens-tah-LAHR ehl POHS-teh tehm-poh-RAH-reeoh.

We need more Romax.
Necesitamos más cable Romax.
neh-seh-see-TAH-mohs mahs KAH-bleh Romax.

We need more conduit.
Necesitamos más conductos/tubos.
neh-seh-see-TAH-mohs mahs kohn-DOOK-tohs/TO-bohs.

We need the conduit bender.
Necesitamos el dobla conducto/tubo.
neh-seh-see-TAH-mohs ehl DOH-blah koh-DOOK-toh/TO-boh.

We need speaker wires in the house.
Necesitamos cables para parlantes en la casa.
neh-seh-see-TAH-mohs KAH-blehs PAH-rah pahr-LAHN-tehs ehn lah KAH-sah.

Are we using fiber-optic cable in this house?
¿Vamos a utilizar cable de fibra óptica en esta casa?
VAH-mohs ah oo-tee-lee-SAHR KAH-bleh deh FEE-brah OHP-tee-kah ehn EHS-tah KAH-sah?

Pull the wire thru the wall.
Jale el cable a través de la pared.
HAH-leh ehl KAH-bleh ah trah-VEHS deh lah pah-REHD.

Where are the wire cutters?
¿Adónde está el cortacables?
ah-DON-deh ehs-TAH ehl KOHR-tah KAH-blehs?

Where is the screwdriver?
¿Adónde está el destornillador/desarmador?
ah-DON-deh ehs-TAH ehl dehs-tohr-nee-YAH-door/dehs-ahr-mah-DOOR?

Where is the hammer?
¿Adónde está el martillo?
ah-DON-deh ehs-TAH ehl mahr-TEE-yoh?

Where is the fuse box?
¿Adónde está la caja de fusibles?
ah-DON-deh ehs-TAH lah KAH-hah deh foo-SEE-blehs?

Where is the conduit bender?
¿Adónde está el dobla conducto/tubo?
ah-DON-deh ehs-TAH ehl DOH-blah koh-DOOK-toh/TO-boh?

Don't touch the shiny red button.
No toque el botón brillante rojo.
noh TOH-keh ehl boh-TOHN bree-YAHN-teh roh-HOH.

We need cable T.V. in the bedrooms.
Necesitamos TV de cable en los dormitorios.
neh-seh-see-TAH-mohs teh-VEH deh KAH-bleh ehn lohs door-mee-TOH-reeohs.

We need cable T.V. in the den.
Necesitamos TV de cable en el cuarto de estar.
neh-seh-see-TAH-mohs teh-VEH deh KAH-bleh ehn ehl KWAHR-toh deh EHS-tahr.

We need to put the ceiling fan in this room.
Debemos colocar el ventilador de techo en esta habitación.
deh-BEH-mohs koh-loh-CAR ehl vehn-tee-lah-DOOR deh TEH-choh ehn EHS-tah ah-bee-tah-seeON.

We need to put can lights here, center first.
Debemos colocar las luces de tarro primero, aquí en el centro.
deh-BEH-mohs koh-loh-CAR lahs LOO-sehs deh TAH-rrroh pree-MEH-roh ehn ehl SEHN-troh.

We need a two gang box here.
Necesitamos una caja metálica para dos enchufes/interruptores aquí.
neh-seh-see-TAH-mohs OO-nah KAH-hah meh-TAH-lee-kah PAH-rah dohs ehn-CHOO-fehs/een-teh-rrroop-TOH-rehs ah-KEY.

We need a three gang box here.
Necesitamos una caja metálica para tres enchufes/interruptores aquí.
neh-seh-see-TAH-mohs OO-nah KAH-hah meh-TAH-lee-kah PAH-rah trehs ehn-CHOO-fehs/een-teh-rrroop-TOH-rehs ah-KEY.

We need a three-way from here to here.
Necesitamos un tres vías desde aquí hasta allí.
neh-seh-see-TAH-mohs oohn trehs VEE-ahs DEHS-deh ah-KEY AHS-tah ah-YEE.

We need to get an inspection.
Debemos obtener una inspección.
deh-BEH-mohs ohb-teh-NEHR OO-nah eens-pek-seeON.

We need to put the debris in the dumpster.
Debemos colocar los escombros en el basurero.
deh-BEH-mohs koh-loh-CAR lohs ehs-KOHM-brohs ehn ehl bah-soo-REH-roh.

We need to clean up the job-site daily.
Debemos limpiar el área de trabajo a diario.
deh-BEH-mohs leem-peeAHR ehl AH-reh-ah deh trah-BAH-hoh ah dee-AH-reeoh.

FLOORS – WOOD/TILE/CARPET
Pisos – madera/baldoza/alfombra
PEE-sohs – mah-DEH-rah/bahl-DOH-sah/ahl-FOHM-brah

How long have you been doing floors?
¿Cuánto hace que trabaja colocando pisos?
KWAHN-toh AH-seh keh trah-BAH-hah koh-loh-CAN-doh PEE-sohs?

I have been doing floors for ___ years.
Hace _____ años que trabajo colocando pisos.
AH-seh _____ AH-neeohs keh trah-BAH-hoh koh-loh-CAN-doh PEE-sohs.

Do you have references?
¿Tiene referencias?
teeEH-neh reh-feh-REHN-seeahs?

Yes, I have references.
Sí, tengo referencias.
see, TEHN-goh reh-feh-REHN-seeahs.

Phrases

No, I do not have references.
No, no tengo referencias.
noh, noh TEHN-goh reh-feh-REHN-seeahs.

Can you give me an estimate for this job?
¿Me puede dar un presupuesto por este trabajo?
meh pooh-EH-deh dahr oon preh-soo-pooEHS-toh pore EHS-teh trah-BAH-hoh?

When can you start this project?
¿Cuándo puede comenzar con este proyecto?
KWAHN-doh pooh-EH-deh koh-mehn-SAHR kohn EHS-teh proh-YEHK-toh?

I can start this job next week/in two weeks.
Puedo comenzar este trabajo la semana que viene/en dos semanas.
pooh-EH-doh koh-mehn-SAHR EHS-teh trah-BAH-hoh lah seh-MAH-nah keh vee-EH-neh/ehn DOHS seh-MAH-nahs.

How long will it take you to complete this job?
¿Cuánto le tomará completar este trabajo?
KWAHN-toh leh toh-mah-RAH kohm-pleh-TAHR EHS-teh trah-BAH-hoh?

It will take a day/week to finish.
Tomará un día/una semana terminarlo.
toh-mah-RAH oon DEE-ah/OO-nah seh-MAH-nah tehr-me-NAHR-loh.

Do you have your own tools?
¿Tiene sus propias herramientas?
teeEH-neh soos PROH-peeahs eh-rrrah-meEHN-tahs?

WOOD
Madera
mah-DEH-rah

We need to lay this floor.
Debemos colocar este piso.
deh-BEH-mohs koh-loh-CAR EHS-teh PEE-soh.

We need to refinish the hard wood floors.
Debemos realizar el acabado de los pisos de madera.
deh-BEH-mohs re-ah-lee-SAHR ehl ah-kah-BAH-doh deh lohs PEE-sohs deh mah-DEH-rah.

We need to sand the floors.
Debemos arenar los pisos.
deh-BEH-mohs ah-reh-NAHR lohs PEE-sohs.

We need three coats of poly on the floors.
Necesitamos tres capas de poliuretano en los pisos.
neh-seh-see-TAH-mohs trehs KAH-pahs deh poh-lee-oo-reh-TAH-noh ehn lohs PEE-sohs.

We want a satin finish on the floors.
Queremos los pisos con una terminación satinada.
keh-REH-mohs lohs PEE-sohs kohn OO-nah tehr-me-nah-seeON sah-tee-NAH-dah.

We need more sand paper.
Necesitamos más papel de lija.
neh-seh-see-TAH-mohs mahs pah-PEHL deh LEE-hah.

We need the edger.
Necesitamos el bordeador.
neh-seh-see-TAH-mohs ehl bohr-deAH-door.

We need to wipe the floor down.
Debemos limpiar el piso.
deh-BEH-mohs leem-peeAHR ehl PEE-soh.

We need clean rags.
Necesitamos trapos limpios.
neh-seh-see-TAH-mohs TRAH-pohs LEEM-peeohs.

Where are the knee-pads?
¿Adónde están los protectores de rodillas?
ah-DON-deh ehs-TAHN lohs proh-tech-TOH-rehs deh roh-DEE-yahs?

Where are the safety masks?
¿Adónde están las máscaras protectoras?
ah-DON-deh ehs-TAHN lahs MAHS-kah-rahs proh-tech-TOH-rahs?

Use the edger to go around the perimeter of the room.
Utilice el bordeador para ir alrededor del perímetro de la habitación.
oo-tee-LEE-seh ehl bohr-deAH-door PAH-rah eer ahl-reh-deh-DOOR dehl peh-REE-meh-troh deh lah ah-bee-tah-seeON.

Where are the mineral spirits?
¿Adónde está el aguarrás?
ah-DON-deh ehs-TAH ehl ah-gwah-RRRAHS?

We need to put paper down after the floor dries to protect it.
Una vez que el piso se seque, debemos colocar papel para protegerlo.
OO-nah vehs keh ehl PEE-soh seh SEH-keh, deh-BEH-mohs koh-loh-CAR pah-PEHL PAH-rah proh-teh-HER-loh.

We can walk on the floors tomorrow.
Mañana podremos caminar sobre los pisos.
mah-nee-AH-nah poh-DREH-mohs kah-me-nahr SOH-breh lohs PEE-sohs.

We need to clean up the job-site daily.
Debemos limpiar el área de trabajo a diario.
deh-BEH-mohs leem-peeAHR ehl AH-reh-ah deh trah-BAH-hoh ah dee-AH-reeoh.

TILE
Baldoza
bahl-DOH-sah

We need to install ceramic tile in the bathroom/kitchen.
Debemos instalar baldoza cerámica en el baño/la cocina.
deh-BEH-mohs eens-tah-LAHR bahl-DOH-sah seh-RAH-me-kah ehn ehl BAH-neeoh/lah koh-SEE-nah.

We need more grout.
Necesitamos más lechada.
neh-seh-see-TAH-mohs mahs leh-CHAH-dah.

We need more tile.
Necesitamos más baldoza.
neh-seh-see-TAH-mohs mahs bahl-DOH-sah.

We need to clean off the grout.
Debemos limpiar la lechada.
deh-BEH-mohs leem-peeAHR lah leh-CHAH-dah.

We need a 5-gallon bucket.
Necesitamos un balde de 5 galones.
neh-seh-see-TAH-mohs oon BAHL-deh deh SEEN-koh gah-LOH-nehs.

We need clean water.
Necesitamos agua limpia.
neh-seh-see-TAH-mohs AH-gwah LEEM-peeah.

We need a clean sponge.
Necesitamos una esponja limpia.
neh-seh-see-TAH-mohs OO-nah ehs-POHN-hah LEEM-peeah.

We need the tile saw.
Necesitamos el serrucho para baldoza.
neh-seh-see-TAH-mohs ehl seh-RRROO-choh PAH-rah bahl-DOH-sah.

We need the grinder.
Necesitamos el molinillo.
neh-seh-see-TAH-mohs ehl moh-lee-NEE-yoh.

Can you cut tile?
¿Puede cortar baldoza?
pooh-EH-deh kohr-TAHR bahl-DOH-sah?

Where is the grout?
¿Adónde está la lechada?
ah-DON-deh ehs-TAH lah leh-CHAH-dah?

Where is the tile?
¿Adónde está la baldoza?
ah-DON-deh ehs-TAH lah bahl-DOH-sah?

Where is the saw?
¿Adónde está el serrucho?
ah-DON-deh ehs-TAH ehl seh-RRROO-choh?

We need to clean up the job-site daily.
Debemos limpiar el área de trabajo a diario.
deh-BEH-mohs leem-peeAHR ehl AH-reh-ah deh trah-BAH-hoh ah dee-AH-reeoh.

CARPET
Alfombra
ahl-FOHM-brah

We need to measure for carpet.
Debemos tomar medidas para la alfombra.
deh-BEH-mohs toh-MAHR meh-DEE-dahs PAH-rah lah ahl-FOHM-brah.

The carpet is on order.
La alfombra ya está pedida.
lah ahl-FOHM-brah yah ehs-TAH peh-DEE-dah.

We need to install the pad first.
Debemos colocar primero el bajoalfombra.
deh-BEH-mohs koh-loh-CAR pree-MEH-roh ehl bah-hoh-ahl-FOHM-brah.

We need to install the tack boards.
Debemos instalar una cartelera/tabla de tachuelas.
deh-BEH-mohs eens-tah-LAHR OO-nah kahr-teh-LEH-rah/TAH-blah deh tah-chooEH-lahs.

We need the hot iron and tape.
Necesitamos la plancha caliente y la cinta.
neh-seh-see-TAH-mohs lah PLAHN-chah kah-leeEHN-teh ee lah SEEN-tah.

We need the carpet stretcher.
Necesitamos el aplanador para alfombra.
neh-seh-see-TAH-mohs ehl ah-plah-nah-DOOR PAH-rah ahl-FOHM-brah.

We need sharp utility blades.
Necesitamos cuchillas de navaja afiladas.
neh-seh-see-TAH-mohs koo-chee-YAHS deh nah-VAH-hah ah-fee-LAH-dahs.

The carpet will be delivered tomorrow.
Mañana entregarán la alfombra.
mah-nee-AH-nah ehn-treh-gah-RAHN lah ahl-FOHM-brah.

Notify me when it gets here.
Avíseme cuando llegue.
ah-VEE-seh-meh KWAHN-doh YEH-geh.

We need to put the carpet in the bedroom/closet.
Debemos alfombrar la habitación/el closet.
deh-BEH-mohs ahl-fohm-BRAHR lah ah-bee-tah-seeON/ehl KLOH-set.

We need to clean up the job-site daily.
Debemos limpiar el área de trabajo a diario.
deh-BEH-mohs leem-peeAHR ehl AH-reh-ah deh trah-BAH-hoh ah dee-AH-reeoh.

FRAMING
Carpintería
car-peen-teh-REE-ah

How long have you been framing?
¿Cuánto hace que trabaja en carpintería?
KWAHN-toh AH-seh keh trah-BAH-hah ehn car-peen-teh-REE-ah?

I have been framing for ___ years.
Hace _____ años que trabajo en carpintería.
AH-seh _____ AH-neeohs keh trah-BAH-hoh ehn car-peen-teh-REE-ah.

Do you have references?
¿Tiene referencias?
teeEH-neh reh-feh-REHN-seeahs?

Yes, I have references.
Sí, tengo referencias.
see, TEHN-goh reh-feh-REHN-seeahs.

No, I do not have references.
No, no tengo referencias.
noh, noh TEHN-goh reh-feh-REHN-seeahs.

Can you give me an estimate for this job?
¿Me puede dar un presupuesto por este trabajo?
meh pooh-EH-deh dahr oon preh-soo-pooEHS-toh pore EHS-teh trah-BAH-hoh?

When can you start this project?
¿Cuándo puede comenzar con este proyecto?
KWAHN-doh pooh-EH-deh koh-mehn-SAHR kohn EHS-teh proh-YEHK-toh?

Phrases

I can start this job next week/in two weeks.
Puedo comenzar este trabajo la semana que viene/en dos semanas.
pooh-EH-doh koh-mehn-SAHR EHS-teh trah-BAH-hoh lah seh-MAH-nah keh vee-EH-neh/ehn DOHS seh-MAH-nahs.

How long will it take you to complete this job?
¿Cuánto le tomará completar este trabajo?
KWAHN-toh leh toh-mah-RAH kohm-pleh-TAHR EHS-teh trah-BAH-hoh?

It will take a day/week to finish.
Tomará un día/una semana terminarlo.
toh-mah-RAH oon DEE-ah/OO-nah seh-MAH-nah tehr-me-NAHR-loh.

Do you have your own tools?
¿Tiene sus propias herramientas?
teeEH-neh soos PROH-peeahs eh-rrrah-meEHN-tahs?

We need more wood.
Necesitamos más madera.
neh-seh-see-TAH-mohs mahs mah-DEH-rah.

We need more nails.
Necesitamos más clavos.
neh-seh-see-TAH-mohs mahs KLAH-vohs.

We need to frame this floor according to the architect's plans.
Debemos construir un armazón/una estructura conforme los planos del arquitecto.
deh-BEH-mohs kohns-troo-EER oon ahr-mah-SOHN/OO-nah ehs-trook-TO-rah kohn-FOR-meh lohs PLAH-nohs dehl ahr-key-TECH-toh.

Can you cut?
¿Puede realizar cortes?
pooh-EH-deh reh-ah-lee-SAHR KOHR-tehs?

We need to fix the soffits.
Debemos arreglar los sofitos.
deh-BEH-mohs ah-rrreh-GLAHR lohs soh-FEE-tohs.

We need to build a deck.
Debemos construir una cubierta/un balcón.
deh-BEH-mohs kohns-TROO-eer OO-nah koo-beeEHR-tah/oon bahl-KOHN.

We need to lap side the rear of the building.
Debemos revestir con tablas con traslapo/solapo la parte trasera del edificio.
deh-BEH-mohs reh-vehs-TEER kohn TAH-blahs kohn trahs-LAH-poh/soh-LAH-poh lah PAHR-teh trah-SEH-rah dehl eh-dee-FEE-seeoh .

We need to trim-out the house after the dry wall is done.
Debemos darle las terminaciones a la casa una vez finalizado el muro en seco.
deh-BEH-mohs DAHR-leh lahs tehr-me-nah-see-OH-nehs ah lah KAH-sah OO-nah vehs fee-nah-lee-SAH-doh ehl MOO-roh ehn SEH-koh.

Where is the hammer?
¿Adónde está el martillo?
ah-DON-deh ehs-TAH ehl mahr-TEE-yoh?

Where are the nails?
¿Adónde están los clavos?
ah-DON-deh ehs-TAHN lohs KLAH-vohs?

Where is the measuring tape?
¿Adónde está la cinta de medir?
ah-DON-deh ehs-TAH lah SEEN-tah deh meh-DEEHR?

Where is the level?
¿Adónde está el nivel?
ah-DON-deh ehs-TAH ehl nee-VEHL?

Where is the laser level?
¿Adónde está el nivel láser?
ah-DON-deh ehs-TAH ehl nee-VEHL LAH-sehr?

The supplies will be delivered tomorrow.
Mañana entregarán los materiales.
mah-nee-AH-nah ehn-treh-gah-RAHN lohs mah-teh-reAH-lehs.

We need to stack the lumber there.
Debemos apilar la madera allí.
deh-BEH-mohs ah-pee-LAHR lah mah-DEH-rah ah-YEE.

We need to frame for a hip roof.
Debemos construir un armazón/una estructura para un techo a cuatro aguas.
deh-BEH-mohs kohns-troo-EER oon ahr-mah-SOHN/OO-nah ehs-trook-TO-rah PAH-rah oon TEH-choh ah KWAH-troh AH-gwahs.

We need to frame for a dormer.
Debemos construir un armazón/una estructura para una ventana vertical de buhardilla/un aposento salidizo.
deh-BEH-mohs kohns-troo-EER oon ahr-mah-SOHN/OO-nah ehs-trook-TO-rah PAH-rah OO-nah vehn-TAH-nah vehr-tee-KAHL deh boo-ahr-DEE-yah/oon ah-poh-SEHN-toh sah-lee-DEE-soh.

We need a gable.
Necesitamos un hastial.
neh-seh-see-TAH-mohs oon ahs-teAHL.

We need to install shake shingles.
Debemos instalar tejas de madera.
deh-BEH-mohs eens-tah-LAHR TEH-hahs deh mah-DEH-rah.

We need to frame for the gutters.
Debemos construir un armazón/una estructura para las canaletas.
deh-BEH-mohs kohns-troo-EER oon ahr-mah-SOHN/OO-nah ehs-trook-TO-rah
PAH-rah lahs kah-nah-LEH-tahs.

Where are the shake shingles?
¿Adónde están las tejas de madera?
ah-DON-deh ehs-TAHN lahs TEH-hahs deh mah-DEH-rah?

We need more scaffolding.
Necesitamos más andamiaje.
neh-seh-see-TAH-mohs mahs ahn-dah-meAH-heh.

We need to frame for a window here.
Debemos construir un bastidor/marco para una ventana aquí.
deh-BEH-mohs kohns-troo-EER oon bahs-tee-DOOR/MAHR-koh PAH-rah OO-nah
vehn-TAH-nah ah-KEY.

We need to get the stairs in.
Debemos colocar las escaleras.
deh-BEH-mohs koh-loh-CAR lahs ehs-kah-LEH-rahs.

What is the pitch of the roof?
¿Cuál es la inclinación del techo?
kwAHL ehs lah een-klee-nah-seeON dehl TEH-choh?

We need the framing nail gun.
Necesitamos la clavadora automática.
neh-seh-see-TAH-mohs lah klah-vah-DOH-rah ah-oo-toh-MAH-tee-kah.

We need the coil nailer.
Necesitamos la pistola para clavos enrollados en tiras/pistola de clavos con tambor.
neh-seh-see-TAH-mohs lah pees-TOH-lah PAH-rah KLAH-vohs ehn-roh-YAH-dohs
ehn TEE-rahs/pees-TOH-lah PAH-rah KLAH-vohs kohn tam-BOHR.

We need to dry this in until the roofer gets here.
Debemos secar esto mientras llegua el techista.
deh-BEH-mohs seh-KAHR EHS-toh meEHN-trahs yeh-GAH ehl teh-CHEESE-tah.

We need to install doors/windows.
Debemos instalar las puertas/ventanas.
deh-BEH-mohs eens-tah-LAHR lahs pooh-EHR-tahs/vehn-TAH-nahs.

That wall needs to be furred out.
Hay que enrasar esa pared.
AHee keh ehn-rah-SAR EH-sah pah-REHD.

We need to plumb this.
Debemos colocarle plomería a esto.
deh-BEH-mohs koh-loh-CAR-leh ploh-meh-REE-ah ah EHS-toh.

We need walk boards.
Necesitamos tablas para caminar.
Neh-seh-see-TAH-mohs TAH-blahs PAH-rah kah-me-NAHR.

We need more support here.
Necesitamos más apoyo aquí.
Neh-seh-see-TAH-mohs mahs ah-POH-yoh ah-KEY.

We need more 2x4/2x6/2x8/2x10.
Necesitamos más de 2x4/2x6/2x8/2x10.
neh-seh-see-TAH-mohs mahs deh dohs pore KWAH-troh/dohs pore SEH-ees/dohs pore OH-choh/dohs pore dee-EHS.

We need a special beam here.
Necesitamos una viga especial aquí.
neh-seh-see-TAH-mohs OO-nah VEE-gah ehs-peh-seeAHL ah-KEY.

We need to get an inspection.
Debemos obtener una inspección.
deh-BEH-mohs ohb-teh-NEHR OO-nah eens-pek-seeON.

We need to clean up the job-site daily.
Debemos limpiar el área de trabajo a diario.
deh-BEH-mohs leem-peeAHR ehl AH-reh-ah deh trah-BAH-hoh ah dee-AH-reeoh.

HVAC
Calefacción y aire acondicionado
kah-leh-fahk-seeON ee EYE-reh ah-kohn-dee-seeoh-NAH-doh

How long have you been working with heating and air?
¿Cuánto hace que trabaja con calefacción y aire acondicionado?
KWAHN-toh AH-seh keh trah-BAH-hah kohn kah-leh-fahk-seeON ee EYE-reh ah-kohn-dee-seeoh-NAH-doh?

I have been working with heating and air for ___ years.
Hace _____ años que trabajo con calefacción y aire acondicionado.
AH-seh _____ AH-neeohs keh trah-BAH-hoh kohn kah-leh-fahk-seeON ee EYE-reh ah-kohn-dee-seeoh-NAH-doh.

Do you have references?
¿Tiene referencias?
teeEH-neh reh-feh-REHN-seeahs?

Yes, I have references.
Sí, tengo referencias.
see, TEHN-goh reh-feh-REHN-seeahs.

No, I do not have references.
No, no tengo referencias.
noh, noh TEHN-goh reh-feh-REHN-seeahs.

Can you give me an estimate for this job?
¿Me puede dar un presupuesto por este trabajo?
meh pooh-EH-deh dahr oon preh-soo-pooEHS-toh pore EHS-teh trah-BAH-hoh?

When can you start this project?
¿Cuándo puede comenzar con este proyecto?
KWAHN-doh pooh-EH-deh koh-mehn-SAHR kohn EHS-teh proh-YEHK-toh?

I can start this job next week/in two weeks.
Puedo comenzar este trabajo la semana que viene/en dos semanas.
pooh-EH-doh koh-mehn-SAHR EHS-teh trah-BAH-hoh lah seh-MAH-nah keh vee-EH-neh/ehn DOHS seh-MAH-nahs.

How long will it take you to complete this job?
¿Cuánto le tomará completar este trabajo?
KWAHN-toh leh toh-mah-RAH kohm-pleh-TAHR EHS-teh trah-BAH-hoh?

It will take a day/week to finish.
Tomará un día/una semana terminarlo.
toh-mah-RAH oon DEE-ah/OO-nah seh-MAH-nah tehr-me-NAHR-loh.

Do you have your own tools?
¿Tiene sus propias herramientas?
teeEH-neh soos PROH-peeahs eh-rrrah-meEHN-tahs?

The unit will be ready to hook up tomorrow.
La unidad/el equipo estará lista/o mañana para conexión.
lah oo-nee-DAHD/ehl eh-KEY-poh ehs-tah-RAH LEES-toh/tah PAH-rah koh-nehx-seeON mah-nee-AH-nah.

We need more sheet metal.
Necesitamos más planchas de metal.
neh-seh-see-TAH-mohs mahs PLAHN-chahs deh meh-TAHL.

Phrases

We need to install the rain guard on the unit.
Debemos instalarle el protector contra la lluvia a la unidad/el equipo.
deh-BEH-mohs eens-tah-LAHR-leh ehl proh-TECH-tohr KOHN-trah lah YOO-veeah ah lah oo-nee-DAHD/ehl eh-KEY-poh.

Check the circuit breaker.
Chequee el interruptor de circuito.
cheh-KEH-eh ehl een-teh-rrroop-TOHR deh seer-KWEE-toh.

We need to run the duct work thru the house.
Debemos instalar los conductos de aire en la casa.
deh-BEH-mohs eens-tah-LAHR lohs kohn-dook-TOHS deh EYE-reh ehn lah KAH-sah.

We need to put in a heat pump.
Debemos instalar una bomba de calefacción.
deh-BEH-mohs eens-tah-LAHR OO-nah BOHM-bah deh kah-leh-fahk-seeON.

We need to put in a gas unit.
Debemos instalar una unidad/un equipo de gas.
deh-BEH-mohs eens-tah-LAHR OO-nah oo-nee-DAHD/oon eh-KEY-poh deh gahs.

We need to install a vent pipe thru there.
Debemos instalar un tubo de ventilación a través de allí.
deh-BEH-mohs eens-tah-LAHR oon TO-boh deh vehn-tee-lah-seeON ah TRAH-vehs deh ah-YEE.

We will use flex duct in the attic/basement.
Utilizaremos un conducto flexible en el ático/sótano.
oo-tee-lee-sah-REH-mohs oon kohn-DOOK-toh flehx-EE-bleh ehn ehl AH-tee-koh/SOH-tah-noh.

We need to hook up the stove for gas.
Debemos conectar el gas a la cocina.
deh-BEH-mohs koh-NEHK-tahr ehl gahs ah lah koh-SEE-nah.

We need to install diverters here.
Debemos instalar desviadores aquí.
deh-BEH-mohs eens-tah-LAHR dehs-vee-ah-DOH-rehs ah-KEY.

Where is the flex duct?
¿Adónde está el conducto flexible?
ah-DON-deh ehs-TAH ehl kohn-DOOK-toh flehx-EE-bleh?

Where is the thermometer?
¿Adónde está el termómetro?
ah-DON-deh ehs-TAH ehl tehr-MOH-meh-troh?

We need vent fans in all bathrooms.

Necesitamos ventiladores en todos los baños.

neh-seh-see-TAH-mohs vehn-tee-lah-DOH-rehs ehn TOH-dohs lohs BAH-neeohs.

How big of an HVAC unit is needed for this house?

¿Qué tamaño de unidad/equipo de calefacción y aire acondicionado se necesita para esta casa?

keh tah-MAH-neeoh deh oo-nee-DAHD/eh-KEY-poh deh kah-leh-fahk-seeON ee EYE-reh ah-kohn-dee-seeoh-NAH-doh seh neh-seh-SEE-tah PAH-rah EHS-tah KAH-sah?

We need to remove the old unit from the house.

Debemos remover la unidad/el equipo viejo de la casa.

deh-BEH-mohs reh-moh-VEHR lah oo-nee-DAHD/ehl eh-KEY-poh vee-EH-hoh deh lah KAH-sah.

What size of a return is needed?

¿Qué tamaño de retorno se necesita?

keh tah-MAH-neeoh deh reh-TOHR-noh seh neh-seh-SEE-tah?

How many feeds come off the unit?

¿Cuántas porciones salen de cada unidad/equipo?

KWAHN-tahs pohr-seeOH-nehs SAH-lehn deh KAH-dah oo-nee-DAHD/eh-KEY-poh?

We need to turn the circuit breaker on/off.

Debemos colocar el interruptor de circuito en encendido/apagado.

deh-BEH-mohs koh-loh-CAR ehl een-teh-rrroop-TOHR deh seer-KWEE-toh ehn ehn-sehn-DEE-doh/ah-pah-GAH-doh.

We need an overflow pan under the unit.

Necesitamos una bandeja recolectora debajo de la unidad/el equipo.

neh-seh-see-TAH-mohs OO-nah bahn-DEH-hah reh-koh-lek-TOH-rah deh-BAH-hoh deh lah oo-nee-DAHD/ehl eh-KEY-poh.

We need to insulate and staple all hard ducting.

Debemos aislar y engrapar todos los ductos duros.

deh-BEH-mohs eyes-LAHR ee ehn-GRAH-pahr TOH-dohs lohs DOOK-tohs DO-rohs.

We need to use diverters here.

Debemos utilizar desviadores aquí.

deh-BEH-mohs oo-tee-lee-SAHR dehs-vee-ah-DOH-rehs ah-KEY.

What is the warranty of the unit?

¿Cuál es el período de garantía de la unidad/el equipo?

kwAHL ehs ehl peh-REE-oh-doh deh gah-rahn-TEE-ah deh lah oo-nee-DAHD/ehl eh-KEY-poh?

We need to put the thermostat here.
Debemos colocar el termostato aquí.
deh-BEH-mohs koh-loh-CAR ehl tehr-mohs-TAH-toh ah-KEY.

What size floor grills are needed?
¿Qué tamaño de rejillas se necesitan para el piso?
keh tah-MAH-neeoh deh reh-HE-yahs seh neh-seh-SEE-tahn PAH-rah ehl PEE-soh?

We need to get an inspection.
Debemos obtener una inspección.
deh-BEH-mohs ohb-teh-NEHR OO-nah eens-pek-seeON.

We need to clean up the job-site daily.
Debemos limpiar el área de trabajo a diario.
deh-BEH-mohs leem-peeAHR ehl AH-reh-ah deh trah-BAH-hoh ah dee-AH-reeoh.

MASON – BRICK/STONE
Albañil – ladrillo/piedra
ahl-bah-NEE-eel – lah-DREE-yoh/pee-EH-drah

How long have you been working with brick/stone?
¿Cuánto hace que trabaja con ladrillo/piedra?
KWAHN-toh AH-seh keh trah-BAH-hah kohn lah-DREE-yoh/pee-EH-drah?

I have been working with brick/stone for ____ years.
Hace _____ años que trabajo con ladrillo/piedra.
AH-seh _____ AH-neeohs keh trah-BAH-hoh kohn lah-DREE-yoh/pee-EH-drah.

Do you have references?
¿Tiene referencias?
teeEH-neh reh-feh-REHN-seeahs?

Yes, I have references.
Sí, tengo referencias.
see, TEHN-goh reh-feh-REHN-seeahs.

No, I do not have references.
No, no tengo referencias.
noh, noh TEHN-goh reh-feh-REHN-seeahs.

Can you give me an estimate for this job?
¿Me puede dar un presupuesto por este trabajo?
meh pooh-EH-deh dahr oon preh-soo-pooEHS-toh pore EHS-teh trah-BAH-hoh?

When can you start this project?
¿Cuándo puede comenzar con este proyecto?
KWAHN-doh pooh-EH-deh koh-mehn-SAHR kohn EHS-teh proh-YEHK-toh?

I can start this job next week/in two weeks.
Puedo comenzar este trabajo la semana que viene/en dos semanas.
pooh-EH-doh koh-mehn-SAHR EHS-teh trah-BAH-hoh lah seh-MAH-nah keh vee-EH-neh/ehn DOHS seh-MAH-nahs.

How long will it take you to complete this job?
¿Cuánto le tomará completar este trabajo?
KWAHN-toh leh toh-mah-RAH kohm-pleh-TAHR EHS-teh trah-BAH-hoh?

It will take a day/week to finish.
Tomará un día/una semana terminarlo.
toh-mah-RAH oon DEE-ah/OO-nah seh-MAH-nah tehr-me-NAHR-loh.

Do you have your own tools?
¿Tiene sus propias herramientas?
teeEH-neh soos PROH-peeahs eh-rrrah-meEHN-tahs?

We need to brick this side of the house.
Debemos colocar ladrillo en este lado de la casa.
deh-BEH-mohs koh-loh-CAR lah-DREE-yoh ehn EHS-teh LAH-doh deh lah KAH-sah.

We need to build a stone wall.
Debemos construir una pared de piedra.
deh-BEH-mohs kohns-troo-EER OO-nah pah-REHD deh pee-EH-drah.

Please bring me more brick/stone.
Por favor, tráigame más ladrillos/piedras.
pore fah-VOHR, TRAHee-gah-meh mahs lah-DREE-yohs/pee-EH-drahs.

We need to level this wall.
Debemos nivelar esta pared.
deh-BEH-mohs nee-veh-LAHR EHS-tah pah-REHD.

We need to mix more mortar.
Debemos mezclar más argamasa.
deh-BEH-mohs mehs-KLAHR mahs ahr-gah-MAH-sah.

We need a 5-gallon bucket.
Necesitamos un balde de 5 galones.
neh-seh-see-TAH-mohs oon BAHL-deh deh SEEN-koh gah-LOH-nehs.

We need clean water.
Necesitamos agua limpia.
neh-seh-see-TAH-mohs AH-gwah LEEM-peeah.

Phrases

We need to clean the grout joints.
Debemos limpiar las juntas de lechada.
deh-BEH-mohs leem-peeAHR lahs HOON-tahs deh leh-CHAH-dah.

Pull the string across the top for a straight line.
Tense el hilo por encima para formar una línea recta.
TEHN-seh ehl EE-loh pore ehn-SEE-mah PAH-rah fohr-MAHR OO-nah LEE-neh-ah RREK-tah.

Where is the level?
¿Adónde está el nivel?
ah-DON-deh ehs-TAH ehl nee-VEHL?

Where is the laser level?
¿Adónde está el nivel láser?
ah-DON-deh ehs-TAH ehl nee-VEHL LAH-sehr?

Where is the mortar?
¿Adónde está el mortero/argamasa/la mezcla?
ah-DON-deh ehs-TAH ehl more-TEH-roh/ahr-gah-MAH-sah/lah MEHS-klah?

The bricks will be delivered tomorrow.
Mañana entregarán los ladrillos.
mah-nee-AH-nah ehn-treh-gah-RAHN lohs lah-DREE-yohs.

We need to stack the bricks here.
Debemos apilar los ladrillos aquí.
deh-BEH-mohs ah-PEE-lahr lohs lah-DREE-yohs ah-KEY.

We need to stack the stones here.
Debemos apilar las piedras aquí.
deh-BEH-mohs ah-PEE-lahr lahs pee-EH-drahs ah-KEY.

Where is the trowel?
¿Adónde está la paleta?
ah-DON-deh ehs-TAH lah pah-LEH-tah?

We need to dry stack a wall here.
Debemos instalar/levantar una pared aquí.
deh-BEH-mohs eens-TAH-lahr/leh-VAN-tahr OO-nah pah-REHD ah-KEY.

We need more scaffolding.
Necesitamos más andamiaje.
neh-seh-see-TAH-mohs mahs ahn-dah-meAH-heh.

Where is the wheel-barrow?
¿Adónde está la carretilla?
ah-DON-deh ehs-TAH lah kah-rrreh-TEE-yah?

How many more bricks are needed?
¿Cuántos ladrillos más se necesitan?
KWAHN-tohs lah-DREE-yohs mahs seh neh-seh-SEE-tahn?

How many more stones are needed?
¿Cuántas piedras más se necesitan?
KWAHN-tahs pee-EH-drahs mahs seh neh-seh-SEE-tahn?

How many more bags of mortar will be needed?
¿Cuántas bolsas más de argamasa/mezcla se necesitan?
KWAHN-tahs BOHL-sahs mahs deh ahr-gah-MAH-sah seh neh-seh-SEE-tahn?

We need to clean the mortar off the brick.
Debemos limpiar el argamasa/la mezcla del ladrillo.
deh-BEH-mohs leem-peeAHR ehl ahr-gah-MAH-sah/lah MEHS-klah dehl lah-DREE-yoh.

We need to get an inspection.
Debemos obtener una inspección.
deh-BEH-mohs ohb-teh-NEHR OO-nah eens-pek-seeON.

We need to clean up the job-site daily.
Debemos limpiar el área de trabajo a diario.
deh-BEH-mohs leem-peeAHR ehl AH-reh-ah deh trah-BAH-hoh ah dee-AH-reeoh.

PAINTING
Pintura
peen-TO-rah

How long have you been painting?
¿Cuánto hace que pinta?
KWAHN-toh AH-seh keh PEEN-tah?

I have been painting for ___ years.
Hace _____ años que pinto.
AH-seh _____ AH-neeohs keh PEEN-toh.

Do you have references?
¿Tiene referencias?
teeEH-neh reh-feh-REHN-seeahs?

Yes, I have references.
Sí, tengo referencias.
see, TEHN-goh reh-feh-REHN-seeahs.

No, I do not have references.
No, no tengo referencias.
noh, noh TEHN-goh reh-feh-REHN-seeahs.

Can you give me an estimate for this job?
¿Me puede dar un presupuesto por este trabajo?
meh pooh-EH-deh dahr oon preh-soo-pooEHS-toh pore EHS-teh trah-BAH-hoh?

When can you start this project?
¿Cuándo puede comenzar con este proyecto?
KWAHN-doh pooh-EH-deh koh-mehn-SAHR kohn EHS-teh proh-YEHK-toh?

I can start this job next week/in two weeks.
Puedo comenzar este trabajo la semana que viene/en dos semanas.
pooh-EH-doh koh-mehn-SAHR EHS-teh trah-BAH-hoh lah seh-MAH-nah keh vee-EH-neh/ehn DOHS seh-MAH-nahs.

How long will it take you to complete this job?
¿Cuánto le tomará completar este trabajo?
KWAHN-toh leh toh-mah-RAH kohm-pleh-TAHR EHS-teh trah-BAH-hoh?

It will take a day/week to finish.
Tomará un día/una semana terminarlo.
toh-mah-RAH oon DEE-ah/OO-nah seh-MAH-nah tehr-me-NAHR-loh.

Do you have your own tools?
¿Tiene sus propias herramientas?
teeEH-neh soos PROH-peeahs eh-rrrah-meEHN-tahs?

We need more paint.
Necesitamos más pintura.
neh-seh-see-TAH-mohs mahs peen-TO-rah.

We need more brushes.
Necesitamos más pinceles.
neh-seh-see-TAH-mohs mahs peen-SEH-lehs.

We need more rollers.
Necesitamos más rodillos.
neh-seh-see-TAH-mohs mahs roh-DEE-yohs.

We need more tape.
Necesitamos más cinta.
neh-seh-see-TAH-mohs mahs SEEN-tah.

We need more drop cloths.
Necesitamos más trapos para limpiar.
neh-seh-see-TAH-mohs mahs TRAH-pohs PAH-rah leem-peeAHR.

We need to get the first coat of paint on the walls and ceilings.
Debemos colocar la primera capa de pintura en las paredes y en los cielorrasos.
deh-BEH-mohs koh-loh-CAR lah pree-MEH-rah KAH-pah deh peen-TO-rah ehn lahs pah-REH-dehs ee ehn lohs see-eh-loh-RRRAH-sohs.

Phrases

We need to strip the old paint off.
Debemos raspar la pintura vieja.
deh-BEH-mohs rahs-PAHR lah peen-TO-rah vee-EH-hah.

We need to sand.
Debemos arenar.
deh-BEH-mohs ah-reh-NAHR.

We need to caulk.
Debemos enmasillar.
deh-BEH-mohs ehn-mah-see-YAHR.

We need to scrape and do the prep work.
Debemos raspar/rasquetear y realizar el trabajo preparativo.
deh-BEH-mohs rahs-PAHR/rahs-keh-tehAHR ee reh-ah-LEE-sahr ehl trah-BAH-hoh preh-pah-rah-TEE-voh.

We need one coat of primer and two coats of base.
Necesitamos una capa de protector y dos capas de base.
neh-seh-see-TAH-mohs OO-nah KAH-pah deh proh-tech-TOHR ee dohs KAH-pahs deh BAH-seh.

We need to scrape the windows.
Debemos raspar/rasquetear las ventanas.
deh-BEH-mohs rahs-PAHR/rahs-keh-tehAHR lahs vehn-TAH-nahs.

Where is the paint for this room?
¿Adónde está la pintura para esta habitación?
ah-DON-deh ehs-TAH lah peen-TO-rah PAH-rah EHS-tah ah-bee-tah-seeON?

We need to wash out the brushes.
Debemos lavar los pinceles.
deh-BEH-mohs lah-VAHR lohs peen-SEH-lehs.

Where are the brushes?
¿Adónde están los pinceles?
ah-DON-deh ehs-TAHN lohs peen-SEH-lehs?

Where are the rollers?
¿Adónde están los rodillos?
ah-DON-deh ehs-TAHN lohs roh-DEE-yohs?

Where are the mineral spirits?
¿Adónde está el aguarrás?
ah-DON-deh ehs-TAH ehl ah-gwah-rrrAHS?

Phrases

We need more rags.
Necesitamos más trapos.
neh-seh-see-TAH-mohs mahs TRAH-pohs.

We need a bucket of water.
Necesitamos un balde de agua.
neh-seh-see-TAH-mohs oon BAHL-deh deh AH-gwah.

We need to clean brushes over here.
Debemos limpiar los pinceles aquí.
deh-BEH-mohs leem-peeAHR lohs peen-SEH-lehs ah-KEY.

We need the extension pole.
Necesitamos el poste de extensión.
neh-seh-see-TAH-mohs ehl POHS-teh deh ex-tehn-seeON.

Where is the extension pole?
¿Adónde está el poste de extensión?
ah-DON-deh ehs-TAH ehl POHS-teh deh ex-tehn-seeON?

We need the ladder.
Necesitamos la escalera.
neh-seh-see-TAH-mohs lah ehs-kah-LEH-rah.

We need to prime this before installing.
Debemos colocarle una capa de protector a esto antes de instalarlo.
deh-BEH-mohs koh-loh-CAR-leh OO-nah KAH-oah deh proh-tech-TOHR ah EHS-toh AHN-tehs deh eens-tah-LAHR-loh.

We need to sand this before the final coat of paint.
Debemos arenar esto antes de colocar la capa final de pintura.
deh-BEH-mohs ah-reh-NAHR EHS-toh AHN-tehs deh koh-loh-CAR lah KAH-pah fee-NAHL deh peen-TO-rah.

We need to caulk here.
Debemos enmasillar aquí.
deh-BEH-mohs ehn-mah-see-YAHR ah-KEY.

We need to touch-up here.
Debemos retocar aquí.
deh-BEH-mohs reh-toh-CAR ah-KEY.

We need to paint the bedroom/kitchen/bathroom.
Debemos pintar la habitación/la cocina/el baño.
deh-BEH-mohs peen-TAHR lah ah-bee-tah-seeON/lah koh-SEE-nah/ehl BAH-neeoh.

We need to put the body color here.
Debemos colocar el color principal aquí.
deh-BEH-mohs koh-loh-CAR ehl koh-LOHR preen-see-PAHL ah-KEY.

We need to put the trim color here.
Debemos colocar el color para la madera moldeada aquí.
deh-BEH-mohs koh-loh-CAR ehl koh-LOHR PAH-rah lah mah-DEH-rah mohl-dehAH-dah ah-KEY.

We need to put the 3rd color here.
Debemos colocar el tercer color aquí.
deh-BEH-mohs koh-loh-CAR ehl tehr-SEHR koh-LOHR ah-KEY.

I will see you tomorrow.
Nos vemos mañana.
nohs VEH-mohs mah-nee-AH-nah

We need to clean up the job-site daily.
Debemos limpiar el área de trabajo a diario.
deh-BEH-mohs leem-peeAHR ehl AH-reh-ah deh trah-BAH-hoh ah dee-AH-reeoh.

PLUMBING
Plomería
ploh-meh-REE-ah

How long have you been a plumber?
¿Cuánto hace que es plomero?
KWAHN-toh AH-seh keh ehs ploh-MEH-roh?

I have been a plumber for ___ years.
Hace _____ años que soy plomero.
AH-seh _____ AH-neeohs keh sohEE ploh-MEH-roh.

Do you have references?
¿Tiene referencias?
teeEH-neh reh-feh-REHN-seeahs?

Yes, I have references.
Sí, tengo referencias.
see, TEHN-goh reh-feh-REHN-seeahs.

No, I do not have references.
No, no tengo referencias.
noh, noh TEHN-goh reh-feh-REHN-seeahs.

Can you give me an estimate for this job?
¿Me puede dar un presupuesto por este trabajo?
meh pooh-EH-deh dahr oon preh-soo-pooEHS-toh pore EHS-teh trah-BAH-hoh?

Phrases

When can you start this project?
¿Cuándo puede comenzar con este proyecto?
KWAHN-doh pooh-EH-deh koh-mehn-SAHR kohn EHS-teh proh-YEHK-toh?

I can start this job next week/in two weeks.
Puedo comenzar este trabajo la semana que viene/en dos semanas.
pooh-EH-doh koh-mehn-SAHR EHS-teh trah-BAH-hoh lah seh-MAH-nah keh vee-EH-neh/ehn DOHS seh-MAH-nahs.

How long will it take you to complete this job?
¿Cuánto le tomará completar este trabajo?
KWAHN-toh leh toh-mah-RAH kohm-pleh-TAHR EHS-teh trah-BAH-hoh?

It will take a day/week to finish.
Tomará un día/una semana terminarlo.
toh-mah-RAH oon DEE-ah/OO-nah seh-MAH-nah tehr-me-NAHR-loh.

Do you have your own tools?
¿Tiene sus propias herramientas?
teeEH-neh soos PROH-peeahs eh-rrrah-meEHN-tahs?

We need to get the water turned on.
Debemos conectar el agua.
deh-BEH-mohs koh-nehk-TAHR ehl AH-gwah.

We need to get the water turned off.
Debemos desconectar el agua.
deh-BEH-mohs dehs-koh-nehk-TAHR ehl AH-gwah.

We need to rough in the house.
Debemos hacer las conexiones de tubería y de electricidad a la casa.
deh-BEH-mohs ah-SEHR lahs koh-nehx-seeOH-nehs deh to-beh-REE-ah ee deh eh-lehk-tree-see-DAHD ah lah KAH-sah.

We need to fix the clog.
Debemos arreglar la obstrucción.
deh-BEH-mohs ah-rrreh-GLAHR lah ohbs-trook-seeON.

How many faucets will there be in the house?
¿Cuántos grifos habrá en la casa?
KWAHN-tohs GREE-fohs ah-BRAH ehn lah KAH-sah?

Are the fixtures in yet?
¿Ya llegaron los artefactos?
yah yeh-GAH-rohn lohs ahr-teh-FAHK-tohs?

We need more copper pipe.
Necesitamos más cañería de cobre.
neh-seh-see-TAH-mohs mahs kah-nee-eh-REE-ah deh KOH-breh.

We need more PVC pipe.
Necesitamos más cañería de plástico.
neh-seh-see-TAH-mohs mahs kah-nee-eh-REE-ah deh PLAHS-tee-koh.

We need to put this faucet in the kitchen/bathroom/laundry room.
Debemos colocar este grifo en la cocina/el baño/la lavandería.
deh-BEH-mohs koh-loh-CAR EHS-teh GREE-foh ehn lah koh-SEE-nah/ehl BAH-neeoh/lah lah-vahn-deh-REE-ah.

We need to dig a new water line in the front yard.
Debemos excavar una nueva canaleta en el jardín del frente.
deh-BEH-mohs ex-kah-VAHR OO-nah noo-EH-vah kah-nah-LEH-tah ehn ehl hahr-DEEN dehl FREHN-teh.

We need to solder that pipe.
Debemos sopletear ese caño.
deh-BEH-mohs soh-pleh-teh-AHR EH-seh KAH-neeoh.

Have you found the leak?
¿Ha encontrado la pérdida?
ah ehn-kohn-TRAH-doh lah PEHR-dee-dah?

Where is the pipe-wrench?
¿Ha encontrado la llave de tubo?
ah ehn-kohn-TRAH-doh lah YAH-veh deh TO-boh?

Where is the shovel?
¿Adónde está la pala?
ah-DON-deh ehs-TAH lah PAH-lah?

Where is the hammer?
¿Adónde está el martillo?
ah-DON-deh ehs-TAH ehl mahr-TEE-yoh?

Where is the propane torch?
¿Adónde está la antorcha de propano?
ah-DON-deh ehs-TAH lah ahn-TOHR-chah deh proh-PAH-noh?

Where is the glue?
¿Adónde está el pegamento?
ah-DON-deh ehs-TAH ehl peh-gah-MEHN-toh?

Where is the septic system?
¿Adónde está el pozo séptico?
ah-DON-deh ehs-TAH ehl POH-soh SEHP-tee-koh?

Where is the pump?
¿Adónde está la bomba?
ah-DON-deh ehs-TAH lah BOHM-bah?

We need to turn the water off at the street.
Debemos desconectar el agua de la calle.
deh-BEH-mohs dehs-koh-nehk-TAHR ehl AH-gwah deh lah KAH-yeh.

We need to put a drain pan here.
Debemos colocar una bandeja de desagüe/drenaje aquí.
deh-BEH-mohs koh-loh-CAR OO-nah bahn-DEH-hah deh deh-sah-GWEH/dreh-NAH-heh ah-KEY.

We need to pull this piping out.
Debemos retirar esta cañería.
deh-BEH-mohs reh-tee-RAHR EHS-tah kah-nee-eh-REE-ah.

We need to get an inspection.
Debemos obtener una inspección.
deh-BEH-mohs ohb-teh-NEHR OO-nah eens-pek-seeON.

We need to clean up the job-site daily.
Debemos limpiar el área de trabajo a diario.
deh-BEH-mohs leem-peeAHR ehl AH-reh-ah deh trah-BAH-hoh ah dee-AH-reeoh.

ROOFING
Techado
teh-CHAH-doh

How long have you been roofing?
¿Cuánto hace que es techista?
KWAHN-toh AH-seh keh ehs teh-CHEESE-tah?

I have been roofing for ___ years.
Hace _____ años que soy techista.
AH-seh _____ AH-neeohs keh sohEE teh-CHEESE-tah.

Do you have references?
¿Tiene referencias?
teeEH-neh reh-feh-REHN-seeahs?

Yes, I have references.
Sí, tengo referencias.
see, TEHN-goh reh-feh-REHN-seeahs.

No, I do not have references.
No, no tengo referencias.
noh, noh TEHN-goh reh-feh-REHN-seeahs.

Can you give me an estimate for this job?
¿Me puede dar un presupuesto por este trabajo?
meh pooh-EH-deh dahr oon preh-soo-pooEHS-toh pore EHS-teh trah-BAH-hoh?

When can you start this project?
¿Cuándo puede comenzar con este proyecto?
KWAHN-doh pooh-EH-deh koh-mehn-SAHR kohn EHS-teh proh-YEHK-toh?

I can start this job next week/in two weeks.
Puedo comenzar este trabajo la semana que viene/en dos semanas.
pooh-EH-doh koh-mehn-SAHR EHS-teh trah-BAH-hoh lah seh-MAH-nah keh vee-EH-neh/ehn DOHS seh-MAH-nahs.

How long will it take you to complete this job?
¿Cuánto le tomará completar este trabajo?
KWAHN-toh leh toh-mah-RAH kohm-pleh-TAHR EHS-teh trah-BAH-hoh?

It will take a day/week to finish.
Tomará un día/una semana terminarlo.
toh-mah-RAH oon DEE-ah/OO-nah seh-MAH-nah tehr-me-NAHR-loh.

Do you have your own tools?
¿Tiene sus propias herramientas?
teeEH-neh soos PROH-peeahs eh-rrrah-meEHN-tahs?

We need to tear-off and dispose of the old roof.
Debemos arrancar y desechar el techo viejo.
deh-BEH-mohs ah-rrrahn-CAR y deh-seh-CHAHR ehl TEH-choh veeEH-hoh.

We need a dumpster.
Necesitamos un basurero.
neh-seh-see-TAH-mohs oon bah-soo-REH-roh.

We need more shingles.
Necesitamos más tejas.
neh-seh-see-TAH-mohs mahs TEH-hahs.

We need more felt.
Necesitamos más fieltro.
neh-seh-see-TAH-mohs mahs fee-EHL-troh.

We need more nails.
Necesitamos más clavos.
neh-seh-see-TAH-mohs mahs KLAH-vohs.

We need more scaffolding.
Necesitamos más andamiaje.
neh-seh-see-TAH-mohs mahs ahn-dah-meAH-heh.

We need to flash around the chimney.
Debemos colocar cubrejuntas alrededor de la chimenea.
deh-BEH-mohs koh-loh-CAR koo-breh-HOON-tahs ahl-reh-deh-DOOR deh lah chee-meh-neh-AH.

Where are the shingles?
¿Adónde están las tejas?
ah-DON-deh ehs-TAHN lahs TEH-hahs?

Where is the felt?
¿Adónde está el fieltro?
ah-DON-deh ehs-TAH ehl fee-EHL-troh?

Where are the nails?
¿Adónde están los clavos?
ah-DON-deh ehs-TAHN lohs KLAH-vohs?

Where is the hammer?
¿Adónde está el martillo?
ah-DON-deh ehs-TAH ehl mahr-TEE-yoh?

Where is the saw?
¿Adónde está el serrucho?
ah-DON-deh ehs-TAH ehl seh-RRROO-choh?

Where is the roofing fork?
¿Adónde están las tenazas para techar?
ah-DON-deh ehs-TAHN lahs the-NAH-sahs PAH-rah teh-CHAHR?

Where is the coil nailer?
¿Adónde está la pistola para clavos enrollados en tiras/pistola de clavos con tambor?
ah-DON-deh ehs-TAH lah pees-TOH-lah PAH-rah KLAH-vohs ehn-roh-YAH-dohs ehn TEE-rahs/pees-TOH-lah PAH-rah KLAH-vohs kohn tam-BOHR?

The shingles will be delivered tomorrow.
Mañana entregarán las tejas.
mah-nee-AH-nah ehn-treh-gah-RAHN lahs TEH-hahs.

Notify me when the shingles arrive.
Avíseme cuando lleguen las tejas.
ah-VEE-seh-meh KWAHN-doh YEH-gehn lahs TEH-hahs.

We need to use shake shingles on this roof.
Debemos utilizar tejas de madera/ripias en este techo.
deh-BEH-mohs oo-tee-lee-SAHR TEH-hahs deh mah-DEH-rah/RREE-pee-ahs ehn EHS-teh TEH-choh.

We need to use 30-yr, architectural shingles on this roof.
Debemos utilizar tejas arquitectónicas de 30 años de durabilidad en éste techo.
deh-BEH-mohs oo-tee-lee-SAHR TEH-hahs ahr-key-tech-TOH-nee-kahs deh TREH-in-tah AH-neeohs deh do-rah-be-lee-DAHD ehn EHS-teh TEH-choh.

We need to use slate on this roof.
Debemos utilizar tejas/pizarras en este techo.
deh-BEH-mohs oo-tee-lee-SAHR TEH-hahs/pee-SAH-rrrahs ehn EHS-teh TEH-choh.

We need to use metal on this roof.
Debemos utilizar metal en este techo.
deh-BEH-mohs oo-tee-lee-SAHR meh-TAHL ehn EHS-teh TEH-choh.

We need to use ridge-venting here.
Debemos utilizar un canal de ventilación aquí.
deh-BEH-mohs oo-tee-lee-SAHR oohn kah-NAHL deh vehn-tee-lah-seeON ah-KEY.

We need to use rubber here.
Debemos utilizar caucho aquí.
deh-BEH-mohs oo-tee-lee-SAHR KAHoo-choh ah-KEY.

What is the pitch of the roof?
¿Cuál es la inclinación del techo?
kwAHL ehs lah een-klee-nah-seeON dehl TEH-choh?

We need to put skylights here.
Debemos colocar tragaluces/claraboyas aquí.
deh-BEH-mohs koh-loh-CAR trah-gah-LOO-sehs/klah-rah-BOH-yahs ah-KEY.

We need to flash around the skylights.
Debemos colocar cubrejuntas alrededor de los tragaluces/las claraboyas.
deh-BEH-mohs koh-loh-CAR koo-breh-HOON-tahs ahl-reh-deh-DOOR deh lohs trah-gah-LOO-sehs/lahs klah-rah-BOH-yahs.

Can you do metal roofs?
¿Sabe cómo trabajar con techos de metal?
SAH-beh KOH-moh trah-bah-HAHR kohn TEH-chohs deh meh-TAHL?

Can you do copper roofs?
¿Sabe cómo trabajar con techos de cobre?
SAH-beh KOH-moh trah-bah-HAHR kohn TEH-chohs deh KOH-breh?

We need to replace the decking here.
Debemos reemplazar la cubierta/el balcón aquí.
deh-BEH-mohs rehm-plah-SAHR lah koo-beeEHR-tah/ehl bahl-KOHN ah-KEY.

We need new decking.
Necesitamos una cubierta nueva/un balcón nuevo aquí.
*neh-seh-see-TAH-mohs OO-nah koo-beeEHR-tah noo-EH-vah/oon bahl-KOHN
noo-EH-voh ah-KEY.*

We need to flash the chimney in copper.
Debemos colocarle cubrejuntas de cobre a la chimenea.
*deh-BEH-mohs koh-loh-CAR-leh koo-breh-HOON-tahs deh KOH-breh ah lah
chee-meh-neh-AH.*

We need to use rubber roofing.
Debemos utilizar techo de caucho.
deh-BEH-mohs oo-tee-lee-SAHR TEH-choh deh KAHoo-choh.

We need to glue the roof down.
Debemos pegar/adherir el techo.
deh-BEH-mohs PEH-gahr/ah-deh-REER ehl TEH-choh.

We need to use drip edge.
Debemos utilizar un canalete de desagüe.
deh-BEH-mohs oo-tee-lee-SAHR oohn kah-nah-LEH-teh deh deh-SAH-gweh .

We need to flash this.
Debemos colocarle cubrejuntas a esto.
deh-BEH-mohs koh-loh-CAR-leh koo-breh-HOON-tahs ah EHS-toh.

We need to install roof vents here.
Debemos instalar ventilaciones de techo aquí.
deh-BEH-mohs eens-tah-LAHR vehn-tee-lah-seeOH-nehs deh TEH-choh ah-KEY.

We need to use ridge vent on the house.
Debemos utilizar un canal de ventilación en la casa.
*deh-BEH-mohs oo-tee-lee-SAHR oohn kah-NAHL deh vehn-tee-lah-seeON ehn
lah KAH-sah.*

We need to tear-off shingles first.
Debemos primero arrancar las tejas.
deh-BEH-mohs pree-MEH-roh ah-rrrahn-CAR lahs TEH-hahs.

We need to use a tarp to catch shingles.
Debemos utilizar una lona para atajar las tejas.
*deh-BEH-mohs oo-tee-lee-SAHR OO-nah LOH-nah PAH-rah ah-tah-HAHR lahs
TEH-hahs.*

Phrases

We need to put shingles and debris in the dumpster.
Debemos colocar las tejas y los escombros en el basurero.
deh-BEH-mohs koh-loh-CAR lahs TEH-hahs ee lohs ehs-KOHM-brohs ehn ehl
bah-soo-REH-roh.

We need to caulk here.
Debemos enmasillar aquí.
deh-BEH-mohs ehn-mah-see-YAHR ah-KEY.

We need to get an inspection.
Debemos obtener una inspección.
deh-BEH-mohs ohb-teh-NEHR OO-nah eens-pek-seeON.

We need to clean up the job-site daily.
Debemos limpiar el área de trabajo a diario.
deh-BEH-mohs leem-peeAHR ehl AH-reh-ah deh trah-BAH-hoh ah dee-AH-reeoh.

Phrases

Notes

The Lingo Guide for Builders
Safety Supplement

Safety is Priority!
¡La seguridad es prioridad!

Information for this section came from OSHA material.
La información de esta sección proviene de material de OSHA.
lah een-for-mah-seeOHN deh EHS-tah sehk-seeOHN
proh-vee-EH-neh deh mah-teh-reeAHL deh UH-shah.

Contact through:
info@thelingoguide.com
www.thelingoguide.com

Published by:
The Lingo Guide, LLC
Nashville, TN

This publication may not be reproduced, stored in a retrieval system, or transmitted in whole or in part, in any form or by any means, electronic or mechanical, photocopied, recorded or otherwise, without the prior written permission of The Lingo Guide, LLC. Copyright ©2006 The Lingo Guide, LLC. All rights reserved.

Table of Contents

The Lingo Guide for Builders is meant solely as a tool to assist in advancing communications between English and Spanish speakers. It is not meant to be used for any legally binding communications nor is the editor, publisher, or author responsible for any errors, omissions, or damages resulting from the use of information contained in The Lingo Guide for Builders.

A

accident free	libre de accidentes	*LEE-breh deh ahk-see-DEHN-tehs*
accident prevention sign	cartel para prevención de accidentes	*kahr-TEHL PAH-rah preh-vehn-seeOHN deh ahk-see-DEHN-tehs*
action plan	plan de acción	*plahn deh ahk-seeOHN*
aerial lift	elevador aéreo	*eh-leh-vah-DOOR ahEH-reh-oh*
ambulance	ambulancia	*ahm-boo-LAHN-seeah*

B

balance	balance	*bah-LAHN-seh*
ball	balón	*bah-LAWN*
bandage	venda	*VEHN-dah*
barricade	barricada	*bah-rrree-KAH-dah*
battery	batería	*bah-teh-REE-ah*
battery charger	cargador de baterías	*car-gah-DOOR deh bah-teh-REE-ahs*
beam	viga	*VEE-gah*
bearer	soporte, almojaya	*soh-POHR-teh, ahl-mo-hay-yah*
blasting	destrucción (con explosivos)	*dehs-trook-seeOHN (kohn ex-ploh-SEE-vohs)*
boom	estampida	*ehs-tahm-PEE-dah*
bracing	refuerzo	*reh-FWEHR-soh*
bridge	puente	*poo-EHN-teh*
buddy system	sistema de asistencia a compañeros/ colegas	*sees-TEH-mah deh ah-sees-TEHN-seeah ah kohm-pah-knee-EH-rohs/koh-LEH-gahs*
bulldozer	nivelador, tractor con pala mecánica	*knee-veh-lah-DOOR, trak-TOHR kohn PAH-lah meh-KAH-knee-kah*

C

capacity	capacidad	*kah-pah-see-DAHD*
cave-in	derrumbe, socavado, desprendimiento	*deh-RRROOM-beh, soh-kah-VAH-doh, dehs-prehn-dee-meEHN-toh*
cement truck	camión de cemento	*kah-mee-OHN deh seh-MEHN-toh*
chutes	conducto, canaleta	*kohn-DOOK-toh, kah-nah-LEH-tah*
cleat	listón, peldaño	*lees-TOHN, pehl-DAH-kneeOH*
clinic	clínica	*KLEE-knee-kah*

combustible	combustible	*kohm-boos-TEE-bleh*
compressed air	aire comprimido	*AH-ee-reh kohm-pree-MEE-doh*
conveyor	portador	*pohr-TAH-door*
counter weight	contrapeso	*kohn-trah-PEH-soh*
crane	grúa	*GROO-ah*
crawl tractor	tractor de cadena/ oruga	*track-TOHR deh kah-DEH-nah/ oh-ROO-gah*
cross bracing	refuerzo en cruz	*reh-foo-EHR-soh ehn krooz*

D

danger sign	cartel de peligro	*car-TEHL deh peh-LEE-groh*
demonstrate	demostrar	*deh-mohs-TRAHR*
derrick	cabría	*kah-BREE-ah*
detonating cord	cable detonador	*KAH-bleh deh-toh-nah-DOOR*
diagonal brace	refuerzo en diagonal	*reh-FWEHR-soh ehn dee-ah-goh-NAHL*
double pole scaffold	andamiaje de doble *caño*	*ahn-dah-meAH-heh deh DOH-bleh KAH-kneeoh*
dozer	excavadora	*ex-kah-vah-DOH-rah*
dust	polvo	*POLL-voh*
dust mask	máscara protectora	*MAHS-kah-rah proh-tehk-TOH-ra*h

E

ear plugs	tapones de oídos	*tah-POH-nehs deh uh-EE-dohs*
electric	eléctrico	*eh-LEHK-tree-koh*
electrical problem	problema eléctrico	*proh-BLEH-mah eh-LEHK-tree-koh*
elevator	elevador	*eh-leh-VAH-door*
emergency contact person	persona de contacto en caso de emergencia	*pehr-SOH-nah deh kohn-TAHK-toh ehn KAH-soh deh eh-mehr-HEHN-seeah*
excavator	excavador/a	*ex-kah-vah-DOOR/DOH-rah*
explosive	explosivo	*ex-ploh-SEE-voh*
eye flush	"limpia ojos" (aparato para ehnjuagarse los ojos)	*LEEM-peeah AUGH-ohs (ah-pah-RAH-toh PAH-rah ehn-whoah-GAHR-seh lohs AUGH-ohs)*
eye protection	protección para los ojos	*proh-tehk-seeOHN PAH-rah lohs AUGH-ohs*

F

| fabricated deck | cubierta pre-fabricada | koo-bee-EHR-tah preh-fah-bree-KAH-dah |

face protection	protección para el rostro	*proh-tehk-seeOHN PAH-rah ehl ROHS-troh*
fall	caída	*kah-EE-dah*
fall prevention	prevención para caídas	*preh-vehn-seeOHN PAH-rah kah-EE-dahs*
fall protection	protección para caídas	*proh-tehk-seeOHN PAH-rah kah-EE-dahs*
fall protection violation	violación a la protección para caídas	*vee-oh-la-seeOHN ah lah proh-tehk-seeOHN PAH-rah kah-EE-dahs*
falling hazard	peligro de caída	*peh-LEE-groh deh kah-EE-dah*
fatality	fatalidad, muerte	*fah-tah-lee-DAHD, moo-EHR-teh*
fire	fuego	*foo-EH-goh*
fire prevention	prevención contra incendio	*preh-vehn-seeOHN PAH-rah een-SEHN-deeoh*
fire protection	protección para incendio	*proh-tehk-seeOHN PAH-rah een-SEHN-deeoh*
first aid kit	botiquín de primeros auxilios	*boh-tee-KEEN deh pree-MEH-rohs ah-oo-XEE-leeohs*
flammable	inflamable	*een-flah-MAH-bleh*
float	flotar, elemento de flotación	*FLOH-tahr, eh-leh-MEHN-toh deh floh-tah-seeOHN*
flying objects	objetos voladores	*uhb-HEH-tohs voh-lah-DOH-rehs*
forklift	montacargas	*mohn-tah-CAR-gahs*

G

gloves	guantes	*GWAHN-tehs*
grader	niveladora	*knee-veh-lah-DOH-rah*
guardrails	barrera de seguridad	*bah-RRREH-rah deh seh-goo-ree-DAHD*
guardrail system	sistema de barreras de seguridad	*sees-TEH-mah deh bah-RRREH-rahs de seguridad deh seh-goo-ree-DAHD*

H

hanger	gancho, colgadero	*GAHN-choh, kohl-gah-DEH-roh*
hard hat	casco	*KAHS-koh*
hard hat area	área de uso obligatorio de casco	*AH-re-ah deh OO-soh oh-bleegah-TOH-ree-oh deh KAHS-koh*
harness	arnés	*ahr-NEHS*
hazard	peligro	*peh-LEE-groh*
hazard communicaton	comunicación sobre peligros	*koh-moo-knee-kah-seeOHN SOH-breh peh-LEE-grohs*

hazard sign	cartel de peligro	*kahr-TEHL deh peh-LEE-groh*
head protection	protección para la cabeza	*proh-tehk-seeOHN PAH-rah lah kah-BEH-sah*
hearing protection	protección para los oídos	*proh-tehk-seeOHN PAH-rah lohs uh-EE-dohs*
help	ayuda	*ah-YOO-dah*
hoist	levantar, alzar	*leh-vahn-TAHR, AHL-zahr*
hoisting and rigging	elevando y apuntalando	*eh-leh-VAHN-doh ee ah-POON-tah-lahn-doh*
hole obstruction	obstrucción/bloqueo en el agüjero	*ohbs-trook-seeOHN/bloh-KEH-uh ehn ehl ah-goo-HEH-roh*
horizontal brace	refuerzo horizontal	*reh-FWEHR-soh uh-ree-SOHN-tahl*
horse scaffold	andamio de caballete/ de burros	*ahn-DAH-meeoh deh kah-bah-YEH-teh/deh BOO-rrrohs*
hospital	hospital	*uhs-PEE-tahl*
hydraulic	hidráulico	*ee-DRAH-OO-lee-koh*

I

illumination	iluminación	*ee-loo-me-nah-seeOHN*

J

jack hammer	taladro	*tah-LAH-droh*
jack	gato	*GAH-toh*
ladder	escalera móvil/ de mano	*ehs-kah-LEH-rah MOH-veel/ deh MAH-noh*

L

lanyard	cordón	*kohr-DOHN*
lever	palanca	*pah-LAHN-kah*
life line	cuerda salvavidas, cerca de seguridad	*koo-EHR-dah sahl-vah-VEE-dahs, SEHR-kah deh seh-goo-ree-DAHD*
lighting	iluminación	*ee-loo-me-nah-seeOHN*
load bearing	soporte de carga	*soh-POHR-teh deh KAHR-gah*
load capacity	capacidad de carga	*kah-pah-see-DAHD deh KAHR-gah*
load line	línea de carga	*LEE-knee-ah deh KAHR-gah*
loader	cargador	*car-gah-door*

M

maintenance	mantenimiento	*mahn-teh-knee-meEHN-toh*
means of egress	salida	*sah-LEE-dah*
means of escape	salida de escape	*sah-LEE-dah deh ehs-KAH-peh*
medical record	historia clínica	*ees-TOH-reeah KLEE-knee-kah*
medical service	servicio médico	*sehr-VEE-seeoh MEH-dee-koh*
misfire	falla	*FAH-yah*

mobil scaffold	andamiaje móvil	*ahn-dah-meAH-heh MOH-veel*
noise	ruido	*rrroo-EE-doh*
noise exposure	exposición	*ex-poh-see-seeOHN*
	al ruido	*ahl rrroo-EE-doh*

O

on-going supervision	supervisión	*zoo-pehr-vee-seeOHN*
	contínua	*kohn-TEE-nooah*
on-going training	entrenamiento	*ehn-treh-nah-me-EHN-toh*
	contínuo	*kohn-TEE-noo-oh*
out-rigger beam	viga voladiza,	*VEE-gah voh-lah-DEE-zah,*
	estabilizadores	*ehs-tah-bee-lee-zah-DOH-rehs*

P

paramedic	paramédico	*pah-rah-MEH-dee-koh*
personal protective	equipamiento para	*eh-key-pah-me-EHN-toh PAH-rah*
equipment	protección personal	*proh-tehk-seeOHN pehr-soh-NAHL*
pipeline	conducto	*kohn-DOOK-toh*
pit	hoyo, pozo	*uh-YOH, POH-soh*
platform	plataforma	*plah-tah-FOR-mah*
pole scaffold	andamiaje de caño	*ahn-dah-meAH-heh deh KAH-knee-oh*
protection	protección	proh-tehk-seeOHN
protection goggles	gafas protectoras/	*GAH-fahs proh-tehk-TOH-rahs/*
	de seguridad	*deh seh-goo-ree-DAHD*
protective frames	marcos protectores/	*MAHR-kohs proh-tehk-TOH-rehs/*
	de seguridad	*deh seh-goo-ree-DAHD*
protective helmets	cascos protectores/	*KAHS-kohs proh-tehk-TOH-rehs/*
	de seguridad	*deh seh-goo-ree-DAHD*

R

rated load	carga calculada	*KAHR-gah kahl-koo-LAH-dah*
reporting	reportar, informar	*reh-POHR-tahr, een-FOR-mahr*
respiratory protection	protección para la	*proh-tehk-seeOHN PAH-rah lah*
	respiración	*rehs-pee-rah-seeOHN*
roll over protection	protección	*proh-tehk-seeOHN*
	de enrolle	*deh ehn-RRROH-yeh*
rope	soga, cuerda	*SOH-gah, KWEHR-dah*
runner	larguero	*lahr-GUEH-roh*

S

| safety belt | cinturón de | *seen-to-ROHN deh* |
| | seguridad | *seh-goo-ree-DAHD* |

safety class	clase sobre seguridad	*KLAH-seh SOH-breh seh-goo-ree-DAHD*
safety contract	contrato sobre seguridad	*kohn-TRAH-toh SOH-breh seh-goo-ree-DAHD*
safety fuse	fusible de seguridad	*foo-SEE-bleh deh seh-goo-ree-DAHD*
safety harness	arnés de seguridad	*ahr-NEHS deh seh-goo-ree-DAHD*
safety inspection	inspección de seguridad	*eens-pehk-seeOHN deh seh-goo-ree-DAHD*
safety net	red de seguridad	*rehd deh seh-goo-ree-DAHD*
safety plan	plan de seguridad	*plahn deh seh-goo-ree-DAHD*
safety poster	poster sobre seguridad	*POHS-tehr SOH-breh seh-goo-ree-DAHD*
safety supervisor	supervisor de seguridad	*zoo-pehr-vee-SOHR deh seh-goo-ree-DAHD*
safety training	entrenamiento sobre seguridad	*ehn-treh-nah-me-EHN-toh SOH-breh seh-goo-ree-DAHD*
safety glasses	gafas de seguridad	*GAH-fahs deh seh-goo-ree-DAHD*
sanitation	sanidad	*sah-KNEE-dahd*
scaffold plank	tablón de andamiaje	*tah-BLOHN deh ahn-dah-meAH-heh*
scaffolding	andamiaje	*ahn-dah-meAH-heh*
scraper	espátula	*ehs-PAH-to-lah*
sewer line	línea de alcantarilla	*LEE-knee-ah deh ahl-kahn-tah-ree-YAH*
shoring	apuntalamiento, equipo de soporte	*ah-poohn-tah-lah-me-EHN-toh, eh-KEY-poh deh soh-PORE-teh*
side rail	larguero lateral	*lahr-GUEH-roh lah-teh-RAHL*
signaling	seÀalización	*seh-knee-ah-lee-sah-seeOHN*
site layout	croquis/diseño de obra/del sitio	*KROH-keys/dee-SEH-knee-oh deh UH-brah dehl SEE-teeoh*
skid pads	rodilleras antideslizantes	*rrroh-dee-YEH-rahs ahn-tee-dehs-lee-SAHN-tehs*

skid plates	placas antideslizantes	*PLAH-kahs ahn-tee-dehs-lee-SAHN-tehs*
slip resistant	antideslizante	*ahn-tee-dehs-lee-SAHN-teh*
slope	pendiente, inclinación, cuesta	*pehn-dee-EHN-teh, een-klee-nah-seeOHN, KWEHS-tah*
soil classification	clasificación del suelo	*klah-see-fee-kah-seeOHN dehl SWEH-loh*
splint	entablillar	*ehn-tah-blee-YAHR*
stairway	escalera	*ehs-kah-LEH-rah*
steel	acero	*ah-SEH-roh*
stilt	pilote	*pee-LOH-teh*
storage area	área de almacenaje	*AH-reh-ah deh ahl-mah-seh-NAH-heh*
suspension rope	cuerda de soporte	*KWEHR-dah deh soh-POHR-teh*

T V W

tie-off	amarra, ligadura	*ah-MAH-rrrah, lee-gah-DO-rah*
top rail	barra/riel superior	*BAH-rrrah / rrree-EHL soo-peh-reeOHR*
trench	zanja	*SAHN-hah*
trench box	caja de trinchera, mula	*KAH-hah deh treen-CHEH-rah, MOO-lah*
tripping hazard	peligro de tropiezo	*peh-LEE-groh deh troh-peeEH-soh*
truck	camión	*kah-meeOHN*
vapor	vapor	*vah-PORE*
ventilation	ventilación	*vehn-tee-lah-seeOHN*
walkway	pasillo	*pah-see-YOH*
wheel	rueda	*rrroo-EH-dah*
window jack	traba para la ventana	*TRAH-bah PAH-rah lah vehn-TAH-nah*
wire rope	soga de alambre	*SOH-gah deh ah-LAHM-breh*
work boot	bota/calzado de trabajo	*BOH-tah / kahl-SAH-doh deh trah-BAH-hoh*
wrecking ball	bola de demolición	*BOH-lah deh deh-moh-lee-seeOHN*

<u>NOTES</u>

Hazards/Peligros

HAZARDS		
PELIGROS		
peh-LEE-grohs		
falls	caídas	*kah-EE-dahs*
trench collapse	derrumbe de zanja	*deh-ROOM-beh deh SAHN-hah*
scaffold collapse	derrumbe de andamiaje	*deh-ROOM-beh deh ahn-dah-mee-AH-heh*
electric shock and arc flash or blast shock	shock eléctrico y arc flash/arc blast shock	*shock eh-LEHK-tree-koh ee arc flash/arc blast shock*
failure to use proper personal protective equipment	falla en el uso correcto del equipamiento para protección personal	*FAH-yah ehn ehl OO-soh koh-RRREHK-toh dehl eh-key-pah me-EHN-toh PAH-rah proh-tehk-seeOHN pehr-soh-NAHL*

Top 10 OSHA Issues

TOP 10 OSHA ISSUES
LOS 10 ASPECTOS BÁSICOS DE OSHA
lohs dee-EHZ ahs-PEHK-tohs BAH-see-kohs deh UH-shah

1. **Scaffolding**
   Andamiaje
   ahn-dah-meAH-heh

2. **Fall Protections (scope, application, definitions)**
   Protección para caídas (alcance, aplicación, definiciones)
   proh-tehk-seeOHN PAH-rah kah-EE-dahs (al-KAHN-seh, ah-plee-kah-seeOHN, deh-fee-knee-seeOH-nehs)

3. **Excavations (general requirements)**
   Excavaciones (requisitos generales)
   ex-kah-vah-seeOH-nehs (reh-kee-SEE-tohs heh-neh-RAH-lehs)

4. **Ladders**
   Escaleras (móviles/de mano)
   ehs-kah-LEH-rahs (MOH-vee-lehs/deh MAH-noh)

5. **Head Protection**
   Protección para la cabeza
   proh-tek-seeOHN PAH-rah lah kah-BEH-sah

6. Excavations (requirements for protective systems)
   Excavaciones (requisitos para sistemas de protección)
   ex-kah-vah-seeOH-nehs (reh-kee-SEE-tohs PAH-rah sees-TEH-mahs deh proh-TEK-seeOHN)

7. Hazard Communication
   Comunicaciones sobre peligros
   koh-moo-knee-kah-seeOH-nehs SOH-breh peh-LEE-grohs

8. Fall Protection (training requirements)
   Protección de caídas (requisitos para entrenamiento)
   proh-tehk-seeOHN deh kah-EE-dahs (reh-kee-SEE-tohs PAH-rah ehn-treh-nah-meeEHN-toh)

9. Construction (general safety and health provisions)
   Construcción (provisiones de seguridad general y de salud)
   kohns-trook-seeOHN (proh-vee-seeOH-nehs deh seh-goo-ree-DAHD heh-neh-RAHL ee deh sah-LOOD)

10. Electrical (wiring methods, design and protection)
    Electricidad (métodos de cableado, diseño y protección)
    eh-lehk-tree-see-DAHD (MEH-toh-dohs deh kah-blehAH-doh, dee-SEH-neeOH ee proh-tehk-seeOHN)

Phrases

BASIC
FRASES BÁSICAS
FRAH-sehs BAH-see-kahs

Safety is priority!
¡La seguridad es prioridad!
ilah seh-goo-ree-DAHD ehs pree-oh-ree-DAHD!

Be safe!
¡Ande con cuidado!
¡AHN-deh kohn kwee-DAH-doh!

We have regular training classes.
Tenemos clases periódicas de entrenamiento.
teh-NEH-mohs KLAH-sehs peh-reeOH-dee-kahs deh ehn-treh-nah-meeEHN-toh.

We have regular safety training.
Tenemos entrenamiento periódico sobre seguridad.
teh-NEH-mohs ehn-treh-nah-meeEHN-toh peh-reeOH-dee-koh SOH-breh seh-goo-ree-DAHD.

We have regular safety inspections.
Tenemos inspecciones periódicas sobre seguridad.
teh-NEH-mohs eens-pehk-seeOH-nehs peh-reeOH-dee-kahs SOH-breh seh-goo-ree-DAHD.

We need a safety class.
Necesitamos una clase sobre seguridad.
neh-seh-see-TAH-mohs OO-nah KLAH-seh SOH-breh seh-goo-ree-DAHD.

We need a training class.
Necesitamos una clase de entrenamiento.
neh-seh-see-TAH-mohs OO-nah KLAH-seh deh ehn-treh-nah-meeEHN-toh.

We use the buddy system.
Utilizamos el sistema de asistencia a los compañeros/colegas.
oo-tee-lee-SAH-mohs ehl sees-TEH-mah deh ah-sees-TEHN-seeah ah lohs kohm-pah-knee-EH-rohs/koh-LEH-gahs.

This is a hard hat area.
Este es un área de uso obligatorio de casco.
EHS-teh ehs oon AH-reh-ah deh OO-soh uh-blee-gah-TOH-reeoh deh KAHS-koh.

This is a blasting zone.
Esta es una zona de destrucción (con explosivos).
EHS-tah ehs OO-nah SOH-nah deh dehs-trook-see-OHN (kohn ex-ploh-SEE-vohs).

All emergency stop buttons are colored red.
Todos los botones de emergencia son de color rojo.
TOH-dohs lohs boh-TOH-nehs deh eh-mehr-HEN-seeah sohn deh koh-LOHR ROH-hoh.

We need to cleanup the job site daily.
Debemos limpiar el área de trabajo a diario.
deh-BEH-mohs leem-pee-AHR ehl AH-reh-ah deh trah-BAH-hoh ah dee-AH-ree-oh..

We have a fire extinguisher.
Tenemos un extinguidor para fuegos.
teh-NEH-mohs oon ex-teen-gee-DOHR PAH-rah FWEH-gohs.

Be careful.
Tenga cuidado.
TEHN-gah kwee-DAH-doh.

Watch out!
¡Cuidado!
ikwee-DAH-doh!

Help me!
¡Ayúdeme!
iah-YOU-deh-meh!

This is a drug free work-site.
No se permiten drogas en este lugar de trabajo.
noh seh pehr-ME-tehn DROH-gahs ehn EHS-teh loo-GAHR deh trah-BAH-hoh.

CRANES
GRÚAS
GROO-ahs

We need a safety class on cranes.
Necesitamos una clase sobre seguridad para grúas.
neh-seh-see-TAH-mohs OO-nah KLAH-seh SOH-breh seh-goo-ree-DAHD PAH-rah GROO-ahs.

We need a safety check on the equipment.
Necesitamos realizar un chequeo de seguridad del equipamiento.
neh-seh-see-TAH-mohs reh-ah-lee-SAHR oon cheh-KEH-oh deh seh-goo-ree-DAHD dehl eh-key-pah-meEHN-toh.

We need to check the load chart.
Debemos chequear el diagrama de carga.
deh-BEH-mohs cheh-key-AHR ehl dee-ah-GRAH-mah deh KAHR-gah.

We need to mark off this area for safety.
Debemos delimitar esta área por seguridad.
deh-BEH-mohs eh-lee-me-NAHR EHS-tah AH-ree-ah pohr seh-goo-ree-DAHD

We need to barricade this area.
Debemos cerrar esta área con barricadas.
deh-BEH-mohs seh-RRRAHR EHS-tah AH-ree-ah kohn bah-rrree-KAH-dahs.

We need to check the wire rope.
Debemos chequear la cuerda de alambre.
deh-BEH-mohs cheh-key-AHR lah KWEHR-dah deh ah-LAHM-breh.

We need to check the chains.
Debemos chequear las cadenas.
deh-BEH-mohs cheh-key-AHR lahs kah-DEH-nahs.

We need to check the hook.
Debemos chequear el gancho.
deh-BEH-mohs cheh-key-AHR ehl GAHN-choh.

We need to watch out for electric lines.
Debemos tener cuidado con los cables eléctricos.
deh-BEH-mohs teh-NEHR kwee-DAH-doh kohn lohs KAH-blehs eh-LEHK-tree-kohs.

We cannot wrap the ropes around the load.
No podemos envolver la carga con las sogas.
noh poh-DEH-mohs ehn-vohl-VEHR lah CAR-gah kohn lahs SOH-gahs.

We cannot move the load over people.
No podemos mover la carga por encima de la gente.
noh poh-DEH-mohs moh-VEHR lah CAR-gah pohr ehn-SEE-mah deh la HEN-teh.

ELECTRICAL SAFETY
SEGURIDAD SOBRE ELECTRICIDAD
seh-goo-ree-DAHD SOH-breh eh-lehk-tree-see-DAHD

We need a training class on electrical safety.
Necesitamos una clase de entrenamiento de seguridad sobre electricidad.
neh-seh-see-TAH-mohs OO-nah KLAH-seh deh ehn-treh-nah-meEHN-toh SOH-breh seh-goo-ree-DAHD.

We need to replace this frayed cord.
Debemos reemplazar este cable que está dañado.
deh-BEH-mohs rehm-plah-SAHR EHS-teh KAH-bleh keh ehs-TAH dah-knee-AH-doh.

We need to locate the electrical lines before digging.
Debemos localizar los cables de electricidad antes de comenzar a cavar.
*deh-BEH-mohs loh-kah-LEE-sahr lohs KAH-blehs deh eh-lehk-tree-see-DAHD
AHN-tehs deh koh-MEHN-sahr ah KAH-vahr.*

We need to install the plates on the switches.
Debemos instalar las placas de los interruptores.
deh-BEH-mohs eens-tah-LAHR lahs PLAH-kahs deh lohs een-teh-rrroop-TOH-rehs.

FALL PROTECTION
PROTECCIÓN DE CAÍDAS
proh-tehk-seeOHN deh kah-EE-dahs

We need a training class on fall protection.
Necesitamos una clase de entrenamiento sobre protección para caídas.
*neh-seh-see-TAH-mohs OO-nah KLAH-seh deh ehn-treh-nah-meEHN-toh SOH-
breh proh-tehk-seeOHN PAH-rah ka-EE-dahs.*

We need to use the lifts to work on.
Debemos trabajar utilizando las alzadas/los levantamientos.
*deh-BEH-mohs trah-bah-HAHR oo-tee-lee-SAHN-doh lahs ahl-SAH-dahs/lohs leh-
vahn-tah-meEHN-tohs.*

We need to put up the guardrails.
Debemos colocar las barreras de protección.
deh-BEH-mohs koh-loh-CAR lahs bah-RRREH-rahs deh proh-tehk-seeOHN.

We need warning lines.
Necesitamos líneas de alerta.
neh-seh-see-TAH-mohs LEE-neahs deh ah-LEHR-tah.

We need to cover floor holes.
Debemos tapar los agujeros del suelo.
deh-BEH-mohs tah-PAHR lohs ah-goo-HEH-rohs dehl SWEH-loh.

We need to use safety nets.
Debemos utilizar redes de seguridad.
deh-BEH-mohs oo-tee-lee-SAHR REH-dehs deh seh-goo-ree-DAHD.

We need to use our safety harness.
Debemos utilizar nuestro arnés de seguridad.
deh-BEH-mohs oo-tee-lee-SAHR noo-EHS-troh ahr-NEHS deh seh-goo-ree-DAHD.

We need another safety harness.
Necesitamos otro arnés de seguridad.
neh-seh-see-TAH-mohs OH-troh ahr-NEHS deh seh-goo-ree-DAHD.

Where are the safety harnesses?
¿Adónde están los arnéses de seguridad?
ah-DOHN-deh ehs-TAHN lohs ahr-NEH-sehs deh seh-goo-ree-DAHD?

We need to wear our hard hats.
Debemos utilizar nuestros cascos.
deh-BEH-mohs oo-tee-lee-SAHR noo-EHS-trohs KAHS-kohs.

FIRST AID
PRIMEROS AUXILIOS
pree-MEH-rohs ah-oo-XEE-leeohs

We need a training class on first aid.
Necesitamos una clase de entrenamiento sobre primeros auxilios.
neh-seh-see-TAH-mohs OO-nah KLAH-seh deh ehn-treh-nah-meEHN-toh SOH-breh pree-MEH-rohs ah-oo-XEE-leeohs.

We need a training class for CPR.
Necesitamos una clase para CPR (resucitación cardio-pulmonar).
neh-seh-see-TAH-mohs OO-nah KLAH-seh PAH-rah seh-peh-EH-rrreh (reh-soo-see-tah-seeOHN kahr-dee-uh-pool-moh-nahr).

We post emergency numbers.
Anunciamos (en lugares públicos) números de emergencia.
ah-noon-see-AH-mohs (ehn loo-GAH-rehs POO-blee-kohs) NOO-meh-rohs deh eh-mehr-HEN-seeah.

Where is the hospital?
¿Adónde está el hospital?
ah-DOHN-deh ehs-TAH ehl uhs-PEE-tahl?

We have a first aid kit.
Tenemos un botiquín de primeros auxilios.
teh-NEH-mohs oon boh-TEE-keen deh pree-MEH-rohs ah-oo-XEE-leeohs.

We need bandages.
Necesitamos vendas.
neh-seh-see-TAH-mohs VEHN-dahs.

Are you hurt?
¿Está herido/a?
¿ehs-TAH eh-REE-doh?

Do you have someone to contact?
¿Tiene a alguien a quien contactar?
¿tee-EH-neh ah AHL-gee-ehn ah KEY-ehn kohn-TAHK-tahr?

Do you need to see a doctor?
¿Necesita ver a un doctor?
¿neh-seh-SEE-tah vehr ah oon dohk-TOHR?

Medical help is coming to you.
Ya llega asistencia médica para Ud.
yah YEH-gah ah-sees-TEHN-seeah MEH-dee-kah PAH-rah oos-TEHD.

Have you had a tetanus shot?
¿Se ha vacunado contra el tétano?
¿seh ah vah-koo-NAH-doh KOHN-trah ehl TEH-tah-noh?

Help is on the way.
Ya llega asistencia/ayuda.
yah YEH-gah ah-sees-TEHN-seeah/ah-YOU-dah.

FORKLIFTS
MONTACARGAS
mon-tah-CAR-gahs

We need a safety class on forklifts.
Necesitamos una clase de seguridad sobre montacargas.
neh-seh-see-TAH-mohs OO-nah KLAH-seh deh seh-goo-ree-DAHD SOH-breh mon-tah-CAR-gahs.

We need a safety check on the forklift before using.
Necesitamos chequear la seguridad del montacargas antes de utilizarlo.
neh-seh-see-TAH-mohs cheh-key-AHR lah seh-goo-ree-DAHD dehl mon-tah-CAR-gahs AHN-tehs deh oo-tee-lee-SAHR-loh.

We need a safety check on the brakes.
Necesitamos chequear la seguridad de los frenos.
neh-seh-see-TAH-mohs cheh-key-AHR lah seh-goo-ree-DAHD deh lohs FREH-nohs.

We need a safety check on the horn.
Necesitamos chequear la seguridad del claxon/la sirena.
neh-seh-see-TAH-mohs cheh-key-AHR lah seh-goo-ree-DAHD dehl KLAK-sohn/lah see-REH-nah.

We need a safety check on the steering.
Necesitamos chequear la seguridad de la dirección.
neh-seh-see-TAH-mohs cheh-key-AHR lah seh-goo-ree-DAHD deh lah dee-rehk-seeOHN.

We need a safety check on the forks.
Necesitamos chequear la seguridad de las paletas.
neh-seh-see-TAH-mohs cheh-key-AHR lah seh-goo-ree-DAHD deh lahs pah-LEH-tahs.

We need a safety check on the tires.
Necesitamos chequear la seguridad de las llantas.
neh-seh-see-TAH-mohs cheh-key-AHR lah seh-goo-ree-DAHD deh lahs YAHN-tahs.

We need maintenance on this forklift.
Necesitamos realizar mantenimiento a este montacargas.
neh-seh-see-TAH-mohs reh-ah-lee-SAHR mahn-teh-knee-meEHN-toh ah EHS-teh mon-tah-CAR-gahs.

We need to remove this forklift from service.
Debemos retirar este montacargas de circulación.
deh-BEH-mohs reh-tee-RAHR EHS-teh mon-tah-CAR-gahs deh seer-koo-lah-seeOHN.

We need to drive slow.
Debemos conducir lentamente.
deh-BEH-mohs kohn-doo-SEER lehn-tah-MEHN-teh.

We need to wear our seatbelt.
Debemos utilizar nuestro cinturón de seguridad.
deh-BEH-mohs oo-tee-lee-SAHR noo-EHS-troh seen-too-ROHN deh seh-goo-ree-DAHD.

We need to check if the rollover structure is in place.
Debemos chequear si la estructura rodante está en el lugar correcto.
deh-BEH-mohs cheh-key-AHR see lah ehs-trook-TO-rah rrroh-DAHN-teh ehs-TAH ehn ehl loo-GAHR koh-RRREK-toh.

We need to check the reverse signal alarm.
Debemos chequear la alarma de marcha atrás.
deh-BEH-mohs cheh-key-AHR lah ah-LAHR-mah deh MAHR-chah ah-TRAHS.

HAZARD COMMUNICATION
COMUNICACIONES SOBRE PELIGROS
koh-moo-knee-kah-seeOH-nehs SOH-breh peh-LEE-grohs

We need a safety class on how to use the Material Safety Data Sheet.
Necesitamos una clase de seguridad sobre cómo utilizar la página de recopilación de datos para materiales de seguridad.
neh-seh-see-TAH-mohs OO-nah KLAH-seh deh seh-goo-ree-DAHD SOH-breh KOH-moh oo-tee-lee-SAHR lah PAH-he-nah deh reh-koh-pee-lah-seeOHN deh DAH-tohs PAH-rah mah-teh-ree-AH-lehs deh seh-goo-ree-DAHD.

We need to use an MSDS for each chemical in the work area.
Debemos utilizar un MSDS para cada material químico en el área de trabajo.
deh-BEH-mohs oo-tee-lee-SAHR oon EH-meh EH-seh deh EH-seh PAH-rah KAH-dah mah-teh-ree-AHL KEY-me-koh ehn ehl AH-reh-ah deh trah-BAH-hoh.

We need to label each container.
Debemos etiquetar cada envase.
deh-BEH-mohs eh-tee-keh-TAHR KAH-dah ehn-VAH-seh.

We need spill clean-up kits where chemicals are stored.
Necesitamos kits de limpieza para derrames en los lugares en los que se almace-nan químicos.
neh-seh-see-TAH-mohs kits deh leem-peeEH-sah PAH-rah deh-RRRAH-mehs ehn lohs keh seh ahl-mah-seh-NAHN KEY-me-kohs.

We need a spill control plan.
Necesitamos un plan para control de derrames.
neh-seh-see-TAH-mohs oon plahn PAH-rah kohn-TROHL deh deh-RRRAH-mehs.

We have a spill control plan.
Tenemos un plan para control de derrames.
teh-NEH-mohs oon plahn PAH-rah kohn-TROHL deh deh-RRRAH-mehs.

We need to use our protective equipment.
Necesitamos utilizar nuestro equipamiento de protección.
*neh-seh-see-TAH-mohs oo-tee-lee-SAHR noo-EHS-troh eh-key-pah-meEHN-toh
deh proh-tehk-seeOHN.*

LADDERS
ESCALERAS (MÓVILES/DE MANO)
ehs-kah-LEH-rahs (MOH-vee-lehs/deh MAH-noh)

We need a safety class for ladders.
Necesitamos una clase de seguridad sobre escaleras móviles/de mano.
*neh-seh-see-TAH-mohs OO-nah KLAH-seh deh seh-goo-ree-DAHD SOH-breh ehs-
kah-LEH-rahs MOH-vee-lehs/deh MAH-noh.*

We need to use the right ladder for the job.
Debemos utilizar la escalera móvil/de mano correcta para cada trabajo.
*deh-BEH-mohs oo-tee-lee-SAHR lah ehs-kah-LEH-rah MOH-veel koh-RRREK-tah
PAH-rah KAH-dah trah-BAH-hoh.*

We need a safety check on the ladder.
Necesitamos chequear la seguridad de la escalera.
*neh-seh-see-TAH-mohs cheh-key-AHR lah seh-goo-ree-DAHD deh lah ehs-kah-
LEH-rah.*

We need to make sure the ladder is clean.
Debemos asegurarnos de que la escalera móvil/de mano esté limpia.
*deh-BEH-mohs ah-seh-goo-RAHR-nohs deh keh lah ehs-kah-LEH-rah MOH-
veel/deh MAH-noh ehs-TEH leem-peeAH.*

We need to mark this broken ladder.
Debemos marcar esta escalera móvil/de mano como dañada.
*deh-BEH-mohs mahr-CAR EHS-tah ehs-kah-LEH-rah MOH-veel/deh MAH-noh
KOH-moh dah-knee-AH-dah.*

We need to use a wooden ladder here.
Debemos utilizar una escalera móvil/de mano de madera aquí.
deh-BEH-mohs oo-tee-lee-SAHR OO-nah ehs-kah-LEH-rah MOH-veel/deh MAH-noh deh mah-DEH-rah ah-KEY.

We need to use a metal ladder here.
Debemos utilizar una escalera móvil/de mano de metal aquí.
deh-BEH-mohs oo-tee-lee-SAHR OO-nah ehs-kah-LEH-rah MOH-veel/deh MAH-noh deh MEH-tahl ah-KEY.

We need to watch out for power lines.
Debemos tener cuidado con los cables de alta tensión.
deh-BEH-mohs teh-NEHR KWEE-dah-doh kohn lohs KAH-blehs deh AHL-tah tehn-seeOHN.

We cannot stand on the top of the ladder.
No podemos pararnos en el escalón superior de la escalera móvil/de mano.
noh poh-DEH-mohs pah-RAHR-nohs ehn ehl ehs-kah-LOHN soo-peh-ree-OHR deh la ehs-kah-LEH-rah MOH-veel/deh MAH-noh.

We need to put the ladder on a solid surface.
Debemos colocar la escalera móvil/de mano sobre una superficie sólida.
deh-BEH-mohs koh-loh-KAHR lah ehs-kah-LEH-rah MOH-veel/deh MAH-noh SOH-breh OO-nah soo-pehr-FEE-see-eh soh-lee-dah.

We need to use a taller ladder.
Debemos utilizar una esclaera móvil/de mano más alta.
deh-BEH-mohs oo-tee-lee-SAHR OO-nah ehs-kah-LEH-rah MOH-veel/deh MAH-noh mahs AHL-tah.

We need to use a shorter ladder.
Debemos utilizar una esclaera móvil/de mano más baja.
deh-BEH-mohs oo-tee-lee-SAHR OO-nah ehs-kah-LEH-rah MOH-veel/deh MAH-noh mahs BAH-hah.

PERSONAL PROTECTIVE EQUIPMENT
EQUIPAMIENTO PARA PROTECCIÓN PERSONAL
eh-key-pah-meeEHN-toh PAH-rah proh-tehk-seeOHN pehr-SOH-nahl

We need a safety class on personal protective equipment.
Necesitamos una clase de seguridad sobre equipamiento para protección personal.
neh-seh-see-TAH-mohs OO-nah KLAH-seh deh seh-goo-ree-DAHD SOH-breh eh-key-pah-meeEHN-toh PAH-rah proh-tehk-seeOHN pehr-SOH-nahl.

We need to wear our safety glasses.
Debemos utilizar nuestras gafas de seguridad.
deh-BEH-mohs oo-tee-lee-SAHR noo-EHS-trahs GAH-fahs deh seh-goo-ree-DAHD.

We need to wear our face shields.
Debemos utilizar nuestros protectores para el rostro.
deh-BEH-mohs oo-tee-lee-SAHR noo-EHS-trohs proh-tehk-TOH-rehs PAH-rah ehl ROHS-troh.

We need to wear our hard hats.
Debemos utilizar nuestros cascos.
deh-BEH-mohs oo-tee-lee-SAHR noo-EHS-trohs KAHS-kohs.

We need to wear our steel toed boots.
Debemos utilizar botas con puntera de acero.
deh-BEH-mohs oo-tee-lee-SAHR BOH-tahs kohn poon-TEH-rah deh ah-SEH-roh.

We need to wear our gloves.
Debemos utilizar nuestros guantes.
deh-BEH-mohs oo-tee-lee-SAHR noo-EHS-trohs GWAHN-tehs.

We need to wear our harness.
Debemos utilizar nuestro arnés.
deh-BEH-mohs oo-tee-lee-SAHR noo-EHS-troh ahr-NEHS.

We need to wear our dust mask.
Debemos utilizar nuestra máscara para el polvo.
deh-BEH-mohs oo-tee-lee-SAHR noo-EHS-trah MAHS-kah-rah PAH-rah ehl POLL-voh.

We need to check our safety glasses.
Debemos chequear nuestras gafas de seguridad.
deh-BEH-mohs cheh-key-AHR noo-EHS-trahs GAH-fahs deh seh-goo-ree-DAHD.

We need to check our face shields.
Debemos chequear nuestros protectores para el rostro.
deh-BEH-mohs cheh-key-AHR noo-EHS-trohs proh-tehk-TOH-rehs PAH-rah ehl ROHS-troh.

We need to check our hard hats.
Debemos chequear nuestros cascos.
deh-BEH-mohs cheh-key-AHR noo-EHS-trohs KAHS-kohs.

We need to check our boots.
Debemos chequear nuestras botas.
deh-BEH-mohs cheh-key-AHR noo-EHS-trahs BOH-tahs.

We need to check our gloves.
Debemos chequear nuestros guantes.
deh-BEH-mohs cheh-key-AHR noo-EHS-trohs GWAHN-tehs.

We need to check our harness.
Debemos chequear nuestros arneses.
deh-BEH-mohs cheh-key-AHR noo-EHS-trohs ahr-NEH-sehs.

We need to check our masks.
Debemos chequear nuestras máscaras.
deh-BEH-mohs cheh-key-AHR noo-EHS-trahs MAHS-kah-rahs.

We need to replace those glasses.
Necesitamos reemplazar esas gafas.
neh-seh-see-TAH-mohs rehm-plah-SAHR EH-sahs GAH-fahs.

We need to replace that face shield.
Necesitamos reemplazar esa protección para el rostro.
neh-seh-see-TAH-mohs rehm-plah-SAHR EH-sah proh-tehk-seeOHN PAH-rah ehl ROHS-troh.

We need to replace that hard hat.
Necesitamos reemplazar ese casco.
neh-seh-see-TAH-mohs rehm-plah-SAHR EH-seh KAHS-koh.

We need to replace those boots.
Necesitamos reemplazar esas botas.
neh-seh-see-TAH-mohs rehm-plah-SAHR EH-sahs BOH-tahs.

We need to replace those gloves.
Necesitamos reemplazar esos guantes.
neh-seh-see-TAH-mohs rehm-plah-SAHR EH-sohs GWAHN-tehs.

We need to replace that harness.
Necesitamos reemplazar ese arnés.
neh-seh-see-TAH-mohs rehm-plah-SAHR EH-seh ahr-NEHS

We need to replace that dust mask.
Necesitamos reemplazar esa máscara protectora del polvo.
neh-seh-see-TAH-mohs rehm-plah-SAHR EH-sah MAHS-kah-rah proh-tehk-TOH-rah dehl-POLL-voh.

SCAFFOLDING
ANDAMIAJE
ahn-dah-meAH-heh

We need a training class on setting up scaffolds.
Necesitamos una clase de entrenamiento sobre el armado de andamios.
neh-seh-see-TAH-mohs OO-nah KLAH-seh deh ehn-treh-nah-meeEHN-toh SOH-breh ehl ahr-MAH-doh deh ahn-DAH-meeohs.

We need to have a training class on the hazards of scaffolds.
Debemos tener una clase de entrenamiento sobre los peligros de los andamios.
deh-BEH-mohs teh-NEHR OO-nah KLAH-seh deh ehn-treh-nah-meeEHN-toh SOH-breh lohs peh-LEE-grohs deh lohs ahn-DAH-meeohs.

We need to set up the scaffold on a solid surface.
Debemos armar el andamiaje sobre una superficie sólida.
deh-BEH-mohs ahr-MAHR ehl ahn-dah-meeAH-heh SOH-breh OO-nah soo-pehr-fee-seeEH SOH-lee-dah.

We need another person to help set up the scaffold.
Necesitamos a otra persona para que nos asista en el armado del andamiaje.
neh-seh-see-TAH-mohs ah OH-trah pehr-SOH-nah PAH-rah keh nohs ah-SEES-tah ehn ehl ahr-MAH-doh dehl ahn-dah-meeAH-heh.

We need to put in the guardrails.
Debemos colocar las barreras de seguridad.
deh-BEH-mohs koh-loh-KAHR lahs bah-RRREH-rahs deh seh-goo-ree-DAHD.

We need to put in the mid-rails.
Debemos colocar las barreras intermedias.
deh-BEH-mohs koh-loh-KAHR lahs bah-RRREH-rahs een-tehr-MEH-deeahs.

We need to put in the toe-boards.
Debemos colocar las tablas para los pies.
deh-BEH-mohs koh-loh-KAHR lahs TAH-blahs PAH-rah lohs pee-EHS.

We need to check the scaffold for damage.
Debemos chequear si el andamiaje está dañado.
deh-BEH-mohs cheh-key-AHR see ehl ahn-dah-meeAH-heh ehs-TAH dah-kneeAH-doh.

We need to wear our safety harness.
Debemos utilizar nuestro arnés de seguridad.
deh-BEH-mohs oo-tee-lee-SAHR noo-EHS-troh ahr-NEHS deh seh-goo-ree-DAHD.

We need to secure our lines.
Debemos asegurar nuestras cuerdas/nuestros cables.
*deh-BEH-mohs ah-seh-goo-RAHR noo-EHS-trahs koo-EHR-dahs/noo-EHS-trohs
KAH-blehs.*

We need to get our safety harness.
Debemos ir a buscar/coger nuestro arnés de seguridad.
*deh-BEH-mohs eer ah BOOS-kahr/koh-HEHR noo-EHS-troh ahr-NEHS deh seh-
goo-ree-DAHD.*

We need to check our equipment.
Debemos chequear nuestro equipo.
deh-BEH-mohs cheh-key-AHR noo-EHS-troh eh-KEY-poh.

We need to have a safety check.
Debemos realizar un chequeo de seguridad.
deh-BEH-mohs reh-ah-LEE-sahr oon cheh-KEH-oh deh seh-goo-ree-DAHD.

We need to have a 10 foot clearance from the electric line.
Debemos tener un espacio libre de 10 pies desde la línea de electricidad.
*deh-BEH-mohs teh-NEHR oon ehs-PAH-seeoh LEE-breh deh dee-EHS pee-EHS
DEHS-deh lah LEE-neah deh eh-lehk-tree-see-DAHD.*

We need to remove that from the scaffold.
Debemos retirar aquello del andamiaje.
deh-BEH-mohs reh-tee-RAHR ah-KEH-yoh dehl ahn-dah-meAH-heh.

Where are the toe-boards?
¿Adónde están las tablas para los pies?
¿ah-DOHN-deh ehs-TAHN lahs TAH-blahs PAH-rah lohs pee-EHS?

Where are the guardrails?
¿Adónde están las barreras de seguridad?
¿ah-DOHN-deh ehs-TAHN lahs bah-RRREH-rahs deh seh-goo-ree-DAHD?

Where are the mid-rails?
¿Adónde están las barreras intermedias?
ah-DOHN-deh ehs-TAHN lahs bah-RRREH-rahs een-tehr-MEH-deeahs?

We need more guardrails.
Necesitamos más barreras de seguridad.
neh-seh-see-TAH-mohs mahs bah-RRREH-rahs deh seh-goo-ree-DAHD.

We need more mid-rails.
Necesitamos más barreras intermedias.
neh-seh-see-TAH-mohs mahs bah-RRREH-rahs een-tehr-MEH-deeahs.

We need more toe-boards.
Necesitamos más tablas para los pies.
neh-seh-see-TAH-mohs mahs TAH-blahs PAH-rah lohs pee-EHS.

STAIRWAYS
ESCALERAS
ehs-kah-LEH-rahs

We need a safety class for maintaining stairways.
Necesitamos una clase de seguridad sobre mantenimiento de escaleras.
neh-seh-see-TAH-mohs OO-nah KLAH-seh deh seh-goo-ree-DAHD SOH-breh mahn-teh-knee-meeEHN-toh deh ehs-kah-LEH-rahs.

We need a safety class on the hazards of stairs.
Necesitamos una clase de seguridad sobre los peligros de las escaleras.
neh-seh-see-TAH-mohs OO-nah KLAH-seh deh seh-goo-ree-DAHD SOH-breh lohs peh-LEE-grohs deh lahs ehs-kah-LEH-rahs.

We need to clean the stairs.
Debemos limpiar las escaleras.
deh-BEH-mohs leem-PEE-ahr lahs ehs-kah-LEH-rahs.

We need to keep the stairway free of materials.
Debemos mantener las escaleras libres de materiales.
deh-BEH-mohs mahn-teh-NEHR lahs ehs-kah-LEH-rahs LEE-brehs deh mah-teh-reeAH-lehs.

We need to install a handrail.
Debemos instalar un pasamanos.
deh-BEH-mohs eens-tah-LAHR oon pah-sah-MAH-nohs.

TRENCHING/EXCAVATION
EXCAVACIONES
EX-KAH-VAH-SEEOH-NEHS

We need a safety class for trench work.
Necesitamos una clase de seguridad sobre el trabajo en las zanjas.
neh-seh-see-TAH-mohs OO-nah KLAH-seh deh seh-goo-ree-DAHD SOH-breh ehl trah-BAH-hoh ehn lahs SAHN-hahs.

Do not enter an unprotected trench!
¡No ingrese en una zanja desprotegida!
inoh een-GREH-seh ehn OO-nah SAHN-hah dehs-proh-teh-HE-dah!

We need a safety check.
Necesitamos un chequeo de seguridad.
neh-seh-see-TAH-mohs oon cheh-KEH-oh deh seh-goo-ree-DAHD.

We need to slope the walls.
Necesitamos darle pendiente a las paredes.
neh-seh-see-TAH-mohs DAHR-leh pehn-dee-EHN-teh ah lahs pah-REH-dehs.

We need to bench the walls.
Necesitamos apuntalar las paredes con tablones.
neh-seh-see-TAH-mohs ah-poon-tah-LAHR lahs pah-REH-dehs kohn tah-BLOH-nehs.

We need to shore the trench walls with supports.
Debemos colocar soportes alrededor de las paredes de la zanja.
deh-BEH-mohs koh-loh-KAHR soh-PORE-tehs ahl-rrreh-deh-DOOR deh lahs pah-REH-dehs deh lah SAHN-hah.

We need to shield the trench walls with the trench box.
Debemos proteger/cubrir las paredes de la zanja con la caja de trinchera/mula.
deh-BEH-mohs proh-teh-HER/koo-BREER lahs pah-REH-dehs deh lah SAHN-hah kohn lah KAH-hah deh treen-CHEH-rah/MOO-lah.

We need another trench box for this job.
Necesitamos otra caja de trinchera/mula para este trabajo.
neh-seh-see-TAH-mohs OH-trah KAH-hah deh treen-CHEH-rah/MOO-lah PAH-rah EHS-teh trah-BAH-hoh.

We need a good way to get out.
Necesitamos una buena salida.
neh-seh-see-TAH-mohs OO-nah BWEH-nah sah-LEE-dah.

We need a ladder.
Necesitamos una escalera móvil/de mano.
neh-seh-see-TAH-mos OO-nah ehs-kah-LEH-rah MOH-veel/deh MAH-noh.

We need some stairs.
Necesitamos una escalera.
neh-seh-see-TAH-mohs OO-nah ehs-kah-LEH-rah.

We need to keep heavy equipment away from the edge.
Debemos mantener el equipamiento pesado lejos del borde.
deh-BEH-mohs mahn-teh-NEHR ehl eh-key-pah-meeEHN-toh peh-SAH-doh LEH-hohs dehl BOHR-deh.

We need to know where the underground utilities are.
Debemos saber adónde están las conexiones de servicios bajo tierra.
deh-BEH-mohs sah-BEHR ah-DOHN-deh ehs-TAHN lahs koh-nehx-seeOH-nehs deh sehr-VEE-seeohs BAH-hoh tee-EH-rrrah.

We need to mark the underground utilities.
Debemos colocarle una marca/identificar las conexiones de servicios que están bajo tierra.
deh-BEH-mohs koh-loh-KAHR-leh OO-nah MAHR-kah/ee-dehn-tee-fee-KAHR lahs koh-nehk-seeOH-nehs deh sehr-VEE-seeohs keh ehs-TAHN BAH-hoh tee-EH-rrrah.

We need to mark the gas line.
Debemos colocarle una marca/identificar la conexión de gas.
deh-BEH-mohs koh-loh-KAHR-leh OO-nah MAHR-kah/ee-dehn-tee-fee-KAHR lah koh-nehk-seeOHN deh gahs.

We need to mark the sewer line.
Debemos colocarle una marca/identificar la conexión de la alcantarilla/cloaca.
deh-BEH-mohs koh-loh-KAHR-leh OO-nah MAHR-kah/ee-dehn-tee-fee-KAHR lah koh-nehk-seeOHN deh lah ahl-kahn-tah-REE-yah/kloh-AH-kah.

We need to mark the water line.
Debemos colocarle una marca/identificar la conexión de agua.
deh-BEH-mohs koh-loh-KAHR-leh OO-nah MAHR-kah/ee-dehn-tee-fee-KAHR lah koh-nehk-seeOHN deh AH-gwah.

We need to mark the electric line.
Debemos colocarle una marca/identificar la conexión de electricidad.
deh-BEH-mohs koh-loh-KAHR-leh OO-nah MAHR-kah/ee-dehn-tee-fee-KAHR lah koh-nehk-seeOHN deh eh-lehk-tree-see-DAHD.

We need to mark the cable line.
Debemos colocarle una marca/identificar la conexión de cable.
deh-BEH-mohs koh-loh-KAHR-leh OO-nah MAHR-kah/ee-dehn-tee-fee-KAHR lah koh-nehk-seeOHN deh KAH-bleh.

We need a soil test.
Necesitamos una prueba del suelo.
neh-seh-see-TAH-mohs OO-nah proo-EH-bah dehl SWEH-loh.

We need a shovel.
Necesitamos una pala.
neh-seh-see-TAH-mohs OO-nah PAH-lah.

Índice

Vocab.

Herr.

Meses, Días, Números

Frases

Notas

Para mayor información,
por favor contacte a:
info@thelingoguide.com
www.thelingoguide.com

Published by:
The Lingo Guide, LLC
Nashville, TN

Esta publicación no podrá ser reproducida, guardada o archivada en ningún sistema de computación ni
transmitida en forma parcial o completa, ya sea por métodos electrónicos o mecánicos, por fotocopias, por medio
de grabación o por cualquier otro método, sin la previa autorización de The Lingo Guide, LLC.
Copyright ©2006 The Lingo Guide, LLC. All rights reserved. v1.4

Dedicado a:
David, Caleb and Silas with love.

Frases-Índice

El propósito de "The Lingo Guide para Constructores" es el de servir
exclusivamente como una herramienta para facilitar la comunicación entre
gente de habla inglesa y gente de habla española. La finalidad de esta guía no
es para que sea utilizada en ningún tipo de comunicado legal. El editor,
publicador y el autor no se responsabilizan por los errores, omisiones o daños
que pudiere causar el uso de la información conentida en "The Lingo Guide
para Constructores".

A

abanico	fan	*fán*
abertura	opening	*óupening*
acabado	finish	*fínish*
acanalado	splined	*ssspláind*
	riffled	*rífeld*
acanaladura de chimenea	chimney chase	*chímni chéis*
acceso	access	*ácces*
accesorio	accessory	*accésori*
acera	sidewalk	*sáid wok*
acero	steel	*ssstíel*
agarradera	handle	*jándel*
aguas negras	sewage	*súech*
agujero	hole	*jóul*
agujero ciego	blind hole	*bláind jóul*
aire libre	open air	*óupen éar*
aislamiento	insulation	*insuléishon*
aislante	insulating	*insuléiting*
alambre	wire	*wáier*
alambre de paca	wire tie	*wáier tai*
albañil	mason	*méison*
alcance	scope	*ssskóup*
alcantarilla	sewer	*súer*
	sewer drain	*súer dréin*
	conduit	*kónduit*
	storm drain	*ssstórm dréin*
alero	eave	*íiv*
alfarje	wainscot	*wéinscot*
	wainscoting	*wéinscoting*
alquitrán	tar	*tár*
alzado	façade	*faséid*
amarre/amarra	binder	*báinder*
	tie	*tái*
ampliación	addition	*adíshon*
anclaje	anchor	*ánkor*
	fastener	*fásener*
andamiaje	scaffolding	*ssscáfolding*
andamio	scaffold	*ssscáfold*
apagador	circuit breaker	*sérkuit bréiker*

	switch	*suích*
aposento salidizio	dormer	*dórmer*
apoyo	support	*sapórt*
areniscas	sandstone	*sándstoun*
argamasa	mortar	*mórtar*
armado	framed	*fréimd*
armadura	truss	*trás*
	reinforcement	*reinfórsment*
armazón	framework	*fréimuerk*
	frame	*fréim*
arrostramiento	bracing	*bréicing*
artefacto	fixture	*fíxcher*
artefacto de iluminación	light fixture	*láit fíxcher*
artefacto del sanitario o baño	bathroom fixture	*bádrum fíxcher*
	plumbing fixture	*pláming fíxcher*
asentamiento	slump	*ssslámp*
áspero	coarse	*córs*
auto cierre	self-closing	*sélf clóusing*
autoridad competente	building official	*bílding ofishal*
azotado	plaster	*pláster*
	plastering	*plástering*

B

bajo piso	subfloor	*sabflór*
baldosa	floor tile	*flór táil*
baldosas cerámicas	ceramic tile	*serámic táil*
banqueta	sidewalk	*sáidwok*
bañera/bañadera	bathtub	*bádtab*
baño	bathroom	*bádrum*
baranda	guardrail	*gárdreil*
	railing	*réiling*
barandilla	rail	*réil*
barra de refuerzo	rebar	*ríbar*
barrote	stud	*ssstád*
base de tejado	subroof	*sabrúf*
bastidor	frame	*fréim*
bastidores de madera	wood framing	*wúd fréiming*
bisagra	hinge	*jínch*

bloque	block	*blók*
bloquear	blocking	*blóking*
boca de acceso	manhole	*mánjoul*
bomba	pump	*pámp*
bombilla	lightbulb	*láitbalb*
boquete	hole	*jóul*
boquilla de rociador	sprinkler head	*sssprínkler jéd*
borde	rim	*rím*
	edge	*éch*
bordes de entablado	sheating edges	*shíting échs*
brazo	bracket	*bráket*
	handle	*jándel*
brea	tar	*tár*
buscador de montantes	stud finder	*ssstád fáinder*
buzón	mailbox	*méilbox*

C

cabezal	header	*jéder*
cabio/cabrio	rafter	*ráfter*
cable conector	wire connector	*wáier conéctor*
cable a tierra	ground wire	*gráund wáier*
cable de extensión	extension chord	*exténshon córd*
cabreada	truss	*trás*
caja de fusible	fuse box	*fiús bóx*
calefacción	heating	*jíting*
calentador	heater	*jíter*
calentador de agua	water heater	*wóder jíter*
	boiler	*bóiler*
calibre	gage/gauge	*géich/góch*
caliza	limestone	*laimstóun*
cámara de aire	air gap	*éar gáp*
camino	walkway	*wókwey*
	path	*pád*
camisa	sleeve	*ssslív*
campanario	steeple	*ssstípl*
canal	gutter	*gáder*
	channel	*chánel*
canalón	chase	*chéis*
candado	lock	*lók*
canilla	spigot	*ssspígot*

Vocab.

cañería	pipe	*páip*
	tubing	*tiúbing*
capa	ply	*plái*
capa base	underlayment	*anderléiment*
	base coating	*béis cóuting*
capa de soporte	underlayment	*anderléiment*
carga muerta	dead weight	*déd wéit*
carpintero	carpenter	*cárpinter*
carril	railing	*réiling*
	rail	*réil*
cartón de yeso	wallboard	*wólbord*
cascajo	gravel	*grável*
cerca	fence	*féns*
cercha	truss	*trás*
cerradura	lock	*lók*
cerramiento	enclosure	*enclóusher*
césped	lawn	*lón*
chapa	sheet	*shít*
chapopote	tar	*tár*
chimenea	chimney	*chímni*
cielorraso	ceiling	*síling*
cimiento/ cimentación	foundation	*faundéishon*
claraboya	skylight	*ssskáilait*
claro	span	*ssspán*
claro de puerta	doorway	*dórwei*
clavija	plug	*plág*
clavo	nail	*néil*
clavo con fuste corrugado	ring shank nail	*ríng shánk néil*
clavo largo para madera	spike	*ssspáik*
clavo sin cabeza	finishing nail	*fínishing néil*
cloaca	sewer	*súer*
cochera	garage	*garách*
código	code	*cóud*
cola	glue	*glú*
colada	lift	*líft*
	sifted	*sífted*
colgadero	hanger	*jánguer*

	hanging	*jánguing*
columna	column	*kólum*
combinación de cargas	load combination	*lóud combinéishon*
compensar	compensate	*kompenséit*
comportamiento	performance	*perfórmans*
	behavior	*bijéiviour*
compresor	compressor	*comprésor*
compuerta	hatch	*jách*
conducto	duct	*dáct*
	conduit	*kónduit*
conducto principal de gas	gas main	*gás méin*
conducto porta cables flexible	flex conduit	*fléx kónduit*
conductos de humo	flue	*flú*
conector	connector	*conéctor*
conector de alambre	wire conductor	*wáier condáctor*
conexión	connection	*conécshon*
	linkage	*línkech*
	fitting	*fíting*
construcción a dos aguas	gable construction	*géibl constrácshon*
constructor	contractor	contráctor
contracción	shrinkage	*shrínkesh*
contrahuella	riser	*ráiser*
contrapiso	subfloor	sabflór
corona (grapas)	crown	*cráun*
costilla	rib	*ríb*
cremallera	rack	rák
	rail	*réil*
cresta	ridge	*rídch*
croquis	layout	*léyaut*
cuadro de cubierta de tejado	roofing square	*rúfing ssscuéar*
cuarto	room	*rúm*
cuarto de baño	bathroom	*bádrum*
cuarto interior	interior room	*intírior rúm*
cuarto de regadera	shower stall	*sháuer stól*
cubierta	decking	*déking*

	cover	cóver
cubierta de azotea	deck covering	dék cávering
cubierta de tejado/techo	roof covering	rúf cávering
cubrejuntas	flashing	fláshing
	batten	báten
cumbrera	coping	cóuping
	ridge	rídch
	ridge cap	rídch cáp
	ridge pole	rídch póul

D

declive	incline	incláin
desagüe	drain	dréin
	drainage	dréinech
desagüe de tejado	roof drain	rúf dréin
descarga	release	rilís
desempeño	performance	perfórmans
desenganchador	release	rilís
desplazamiento	offset	ófset
destino	occupancy	ókiupansi
desvío	offset	ófset
detector de humo	smoke detector	sssmóuk ditéctor
dibujos	working drawings	wérking dróings
dintel (de la puerta)	lintel	líntel
	header	jéder
diseño	layout	léyaut
dispositivo de traba	latching device	láching diváis
división	partition	partíshon
ducha	shower	sháuer

E

edificación	building	bílding
electricidad	electricity	electríciti
electricista	electrician	electríshan
elevador	elevator	elevéitor
eliminación	removal	remúval
empalme	junction	chánkshon
	splice	sssspláis
empanelado	paneling	páneling
empaque	gasket	gásket
empaque de cera	wax seal	wáx síel

encerrado	enclosed	*enclóusd*
enchufe	electrical outlet	eléctrical *áutlet*
	plug	*plág*
enclavamiento	interlocking	*interlóking*
encofrado	formwork	*fórmwerk*
encofrados	forms (concrete)	*fórms (cónkrit)*
encogimiento	shrinkage	*shrínkech*
enlace	link	*línk*
	linkage	*línkech*
enlucido	plaster	*pláster*
	plastering	*plástering*
enrasado	furred out	*férrd áut*
entablado	sheathing	*shíding*
entablonado	planking	*plánking*
entarimado de tejado	roof sheeting	*rúf shíting*
entrada	entrance	*éntrans*
	doorway	*dórwei*
escalera	stairway	ssstéarwei
	stairs	*ssstéars*
escalera de mano	ladder	*láder*
escalones	steps	*ssstéps*
escape	exhaust	*exóst*
escombro	rubble	*rábl*
esfuerzo	stress	ssstrés
espacio angosto	crawl space	*cról ssspéis*
espiga	spigot	*ssspígot*
estribo para vigueta	joist hangers	*chóist jánguer*
estructura	frame	*fréim*
	structure	ssstrácter
estuco	stucco	*ssstúko*
estufa	stove	*ssstóuv*
	heater	*jíter*
excavar	dig	*díg*
excusado	toilet	*tóilet*
extracción	exhaust	*exóst*

F

fachada	façade	*faséid*
fieltro	felt	*félt*
fijadores	restraints	*ristréints*

Vocab.

fluorescente	fluorescent	*fluorésent*
foco	light bulb	*láit bálb*
foco industrial	floodlight	*flódlait*
fontanero/plomero	plumber	*plámer*
forjados	plastering	*plástering*
fregadero de cocina	kitchen sink	*kíchen sínk*
friso	wainscot	*wéinscot*
función	occupancy	*ókiupansi*
fundación	foundation	*faundéishon*
fusible	fuse	*fiús*

G

gancho	hanger	*jánguer*
garage	garage	*garách*
gases	fumes	*fiúms*
gotera	gutter	*gáder*
grava	gravel	*grável*
grifo de manguera	sill cock	*síl cók*
grueso	thick	*dík*
guarnición	curb	*kérb*

H

habitación	dwelling	*duéling*
	room	*rúm*
hastial	gable	*géibl*
herramienta	tool	*túl*
hormigón	concrete	*cónkrit*
hormigonada	lift	*líft*
hoyo	hole	*jóul*
humo	smoke	*sssmóuk*

I

imprimado	primed	*práimd*
imprimador	primer	*práimer*
inclinación	incline	*incláin*
indicador	gage/gauge	*géich/góch*
ingeniero	engineer	*encheníer*
inodoro	toilet	*tóilet*
instalación en obra	rough-in	*ráf-in*
instalaciones hidráulicas/ sanitarias	plumbing	*pláming*
interruptor	switch	*suích*

Vocab.

interruptor principal	main breaker	*méin bréiker*
interruptor fusible	ground fault	*gráund fólt*
de seguridad	circuit	*sérkuit*
a tierra		

J

jácena	girder	*guérder*
jaharro	plaster	*pláster*
	plastering	*plástering*
junta	joint	*chóint*

L

ladera	incline	*incláin*
ladrillo cerámico	masonry tile	*másonry táil*
ladrillo para frentes	facing brick	*féising brik*
lámina	sheeting	*shíting*
laminado	sheet metal	*shít métal*
lámpara	flashlight	*fláshlait*
larguero	runner	*ráner*
	stringer	*ssstrínguer*
lavabo	sink	*sínk*
lavadora y secadora	washer and dryer	*wásher and dráier*
lechada de cemento	grout	*gráut*
levantamiento	lift	*líft*
liberación	release	*rilís*
lindero	property line	*próperti láin*
línea de gis/marcar	chalk line	*chólk láin*
línea de propiedad	property line	*próperti láin*
listón	strip	*ssstrip*
listón para clavar	nailing strip	*néiling ssstrip*
llave (plomería)	faucet	*fóset*
	spigot	*ssspigót*
llave de alivio	relief valve	*relíf válv*
losa	slab	*ssslláb*
lote	lot	*lót*
	lift	*líft*
luz	light	*láit*

M

machilhembrado	tongue and groove	*tang and grúv*
madera aglomerada	particle board	*párticl bórd*
madera de	timber	*tímber*

Vocab.

construcción	lumber	*lámber*
madera prensada	plywood	*pláiwud*
madera tratada	treated wood	*tríted wúd*
mampara de ducha	shower door	*sháuer dór*
mampostería	masonry	*másonri*
mampostería reforzada	reinforced masonry	*reinfórsd másonri*
manga	sleeve	*ssslív*
manguera	hose	*jóus*
manipular	handle	*jándel*
manómetro	gage/gauge	*géich/góch*
marco	frame	*fréim*
marco de puerta	doorframe	*dór fréim*
marco de ventana	window frame	*window fréim*
enmasillado, enmasillar	caulking, caulk	*cóking, cók*
mastique	mastic	*mastíc*
material de revestimiento	wainscoting	*wéinscoting*
material para pisos	flooring	*flóring*
matriz	main	*méin*
mediera	fence	*féns*
medidor	meter	*míter*
mezcla	mortar	*mórtar*
mingitorio	urinal	*iúrinal*
moldura	molding	*móulding*
	trim	*trím*
montante	stud	*ssstád*
	gable stud	*géibl ssstád*
montante de acero	steel stud	*ssstíel ssstád*
morsa	vise	*váis*
mortero	mortar	*mórtar*
mortero de cemento	grout	*gráut*
museca	rabbet	*rábet*
	chase	*chéis*
muro	wall	*wól*
muro con montantes	stud wall	*ssstád wól*
muro de carga	bearing wall	*béaring wól*
muro de fundacion	foundation wall	*faundéishon wól*
muro en seco	dry wall	*dráiwol*

Español	English	Pronunciación
muro exterior	exterior wall	*extírior wól*
muros rajados	cracked walls	*crákd wóls*

N

nivelación	grading	*gréiding*

O

obra	work	*wérk*
	field	*fíeld*
ojal	grommet	*grómet*

P

panel	board	*bórd*
panel de yeso	gypsum board	*chípsom bórd*
	gypsum wallboard	*chípsom wálbord*
papel de brea	tar paper	*tár péipar*
parante	stud	*ssstád*
parcela	property	*próperti*
	parcel	*párcel*
pared	wall	*wól*
pared exterior	exterior wall	*extírior wól*
pared de barrotes	stud wall	*ssstád wól*
pasamano	handrail	*jándreil*
pasillo	passageway	*pásechwey*
	hallway	*jólwey*
pasta de muro	joint compound	*chóint cómpaund*
	taping compound	*téiping cómpaund*
pasto	lawn	*lón*
	grass	*grás*
pavimento	pavement	*péivment*
peldaños	steps	*ssstéps*
peligroso	hazardous	*jásardous*
	dangerous	déinchoros
pendiente	slope	*ssslóup*
	incline	incláin
perforación	drilling	*dríling*
permiso (de construcción)	permit	*pérmit*
perno de expansión	expansion bolt	*expánshon bólt*
perno de seguridad	lock bolt	*lók bólt*
piedra	rock	*rók*
	stone	*ssstóun*
pieza de inflexión	offset	*ófset*

Vocab.

pileta de cocina	kitchen sink	*kíchen sínk*
pilotes	piles	*páils*
pintor	painter	*péinter*
piso	floor	*flór*
	store	*ssstór*
piso cerámico	ceramic tile	*serámic táil*
placa de cartela/ unión	gusset plate	*gáset pléit*
placa del interruptor	switch plate	*suích pléit*
plafón de yeso	gypsum board	*chípsom bórd*
plancha	sheet	*shít*
plancha de escurrimiento	flashing	*fláshing*
planchuela de perno	washer	*wásher*
planos	design drawings	*disáin dróings*
	working drawings	*wérking dróings*
planta baja	ground level	*gráund level*
plataforma	floor deck	*flór dék*
plataforma de carga	pallet	*pálet*
plataforma metálica	metal deck	*métal dék*
pliego	sheet	*shít*
portal	doorway	*dórwei*
portátil	portable	*pórtabl*
pórtico	frame	*fréim*
postes	poles	*póuls*
	posts	*póusts*
presión	pressure	*préshor*
principal	main	*méin*
privado	private	*práivet*
propiedad	property	*próperti*
proporción	rate	*réit*
	proportion	*propórshon*
provisional	temporary	*témporari*
puerta	door	*dór*
puerta pivotante	swinging door	*swínguing dór*
puntales de refuerzo	bridging	*bríching*

R

rajaduras	cracks	*cráks*
rasante	grade	*gréid*
rebaje a media	shiplap	*shíplap*

Vocab.

madera		
recinto	shaft	*sháft*
recinto de escaleras	stairwells	*ssstéarwels*
	enclosed stairway	*enclóusd ssstéarwei*
recubrimiento	cover	*cáver*
	lining	*láining*
reducción	shrinkage	*shrínkeich*
refuerzo	reinforcement	*reinfórsment*
	stiffener	*ssstífener*
regadera	shower head	*sháuer jéd*
	shower stall	*sháuer stól*
regulador	damper	*dámper*
	regulator	*reguiuléitor*
reja/rejilla	grille	*gríl*
rejilla de piso	baseboard register	*béisbord réchister*
rellenado	filled	*fíld*
relleno	backfill	*bákfil*
remache	rivet	*rívet*
remoción	removal	*remúval*
reparación/reparo	repair	*ripéar*
repello	plastering	*plástering*
repisa	shelf	*shélf*
repisa de ventana	window sill	*window síl*
resaltar	set out	*sét áut*
residencia	dwelling	*duéling*
	residence	*résidens*
respiradero	vent	*vent*
respiradero matriz	main vent	*méin vent*
respiradero vertical	vent stack	*vent sssták*
reticulado	truss	*trás*
retiro	setback	*sétbak*
retrete	toilet	*tóilet*
revestimiento	siding	*sáiding*
	facing	*féising*
revestimiento de vinilo	vinyl siding	*váinil sáiding*
revoque	plaster	*pláster*
	stucco	*ssstúko*
revoque de yeso	gypsum plaster	*chípsom pláster*
riel de guía	guide rail	*gáid réil*

Vocab

ripia	wood shingle/ shake	*wúd shínguel/ shéik*
ripio	gravel	*grável*
roca	rock	*rók*
	stone	*ssstóun*
rociador	sprinkler	*ssssprínkler*

S

salida	exit	*éxit*
sanitario	restroom	*réstrum*
	bathroom	*bádrum*
	toilet	*tóilet*
selladores	sealants	*sílants*
sensor de humo	smoke detector	*ssssmóuk ditéctor*
separación	partition	*partíshon*
sin plomo	lead free	*led frí*
sistema de extracción de humo	smoke exhaust system	*ssssmóuk exóst sístem*
sistema de rociadores	sprinkler system	*ssssprínkler sístem*
sistema doble	dual system	*dúal sístem*
sitio	premises	*prémises*
	site	*sáit*
sobresolape	overlap	*óuverlap*
sobrestante	supervisor	*supervásor*
sofito	soffit	*sófit*
soldadura	welding	*wélding*
solera doble	double plate	*dábl pléit*
solera inferior	sill plate	*síl pléit*
soplete	soldering torch	*sóldering tórch*
soporte	support	*sapórt*
	backing	*báking*
soporte de ventana	window sill	*wíndow síl*
sótano	basement	*béisment*
subpiso	subfloor	*sabflór*
substrato	underlayment	*anderléiment*
supervisor	supervisor	*supervásor*
	inspector	*inspéctor*

T

tabique	partition	*partíshon*

tabique movible	movable partition	*múvabol partíshon*
tabla	board	*bórd*
tabla de cumbrera	ridge board	*rídch bórd*
tabla de pie	tote board	*tóut bórd*
tablero de yeso	gypsum board	*chípsom bórd*
	dry wall	*drái wól*
tablero duro	hardboard	*járd bórd*
	plywood	*pláiwud*
tablón	plank	*plánk*
talud	slope	*ssslóup*
tapajuntas	flashing	*fláshing*
tapanco	attic	*átic*
tejado	roofing	*rúfing*
	ceiling	*síling*
tejado a dos aguas	gable roof	*géibl rúf*
tejado a cuatro aguas	hip roof	*jíp rúf*
tejado en pendiente	slope roof	*slóup rúf*
tejado plano	flat roof	*flát rúf*
teja	shingle	*shínguel*
teja de asfalto	asphalt shingle	*ásfalt shínguel*
teja de madera	wood shake shingle	*wúd sheik shínguel*
teja de pizarra	slate shingle	*sssléit shínguel*
tenencia	occupancy	*ókiupansi*
	stress	*ssstrés*
terminación de la obra	completion of work	*complíshon ov wérk*
terminar	finish	*fínish*
termita	termite	*térmait*
termotanque	water heater	*wóder jíter*
terreno	lot	*lót*
tiras metálicas	stripping	*ssstríping*
tomacorriente/ enchufe	power outlet	*páuer áutlet*
tornillo	screw	*ssscrú*
	bolt	*bóult*
trabajo	work	*wérk*
trabar	block	*blók*
	bolt	*bóult*

Vocab.

trabas	blocks	*blóks*
tragaluz	skylight	*ssskáilait*
trazar y nivelar	line and grade	*láin ánd gréid*
tubería	tubing	*tiúbing*
	piping	*páiping*
tubería principal	water main	*wóder méin*
tubo	pipe	*páip*
tubo vertical	riser pipe	*ráiser páip*

U

umbral	door sill	*dór síl*
	threshold	*dréshould*
unión	joint	*chóint*
	union	*iúnion*
urinal/urinado	urinal	*iúrinal*
uso	use	*iús*

V

vacío	vacuum	*váquium*
valor	value	*váliu*
válvula de alivio	relief valve	*relíf válv*
válvula de cierre	shutoff valve	*shátof válv*
vano	span	*ssspán*
varilla	rebar	*ríbar*
varillas en aro	ringed shanks	*ríngd shánks*
ventana	window	*wíndow*
ventilador	fan	*fán*
vereda	pathway	*pádwey*
vestíbulo	vestibule	*véstibiul*
vidriado	glazed	*gléisd*
	glazing	*gléising*
vierteaguas	flashing	*fláshing*
viga	joist	*chóist*
	beam	*bím*
viga de carga	load bearing joist	*lóud béaring chóist*
vigueta	joist	*chóist*
vigueta de piso	floor joist	*flór chóist*
vivienda	dwelling	*duéling*
voladizo	overhang	*óuverjang*
	cantilever	*cantiléver*
voltaje	voltage	*vóltech*
voltios	volts	*vólts*

| vuelo | overhang | *óuverjang* |
| vuelos | nosings | *nóusings* |

Y

| yerbajos/ yerbas | weeds | *wíds* |
| yeso | plaster | *pláster* |

Z

zapata	footing	*fúting*
zapatilla eléctrica	power strip	*páuer ssstrip*
zarpa	footing	*fúting*
zócalo	baseboard	*béisbord*
zona	zone	*zóun*

LAS HERRAMIENTAS
TOOLS
Túls

alicates	pliers	*pláiers*
alicates de extensión/presión	channel lock pliers	*chánel lók pláiers*
aplanadora	roller	*róuler*
azadón	hoe	*jóu*
bomba	pump	*pámp*
botador/embutidor	nail set	*néil sét*
botiquín	medicine cabinet	*médisin cábinet*
	first aid kit	*férst éid kit*
barreno	drill bit	*dril bit*
buriladora	router	*ráuder*
burro	sawhorse	*sójors*
caja de corte en ángulos	mitre box	*máiter bóx*
caja de herramientas	tool box	*túl bóx*
careta para soldar	welding box	*wélding bóx*
carretilla/carrucha	wheelbarrow	*wíelbarrou*
cepillo	plane	*pléin*
cepillo automático	joiner	*chóiner*
cincel	chisel	*chísel*
clavadora automática	nail gun	*néil gan*
contorneador	router	*ráuder*
cortacésped	lawnmower	*lónmower*
cortapluma	utility knife	*iutílity náif*

cubeta	bucket	*báket*
desarmador/ destornillador	screwdriver	*ssscrúdráiver*
desarmador/ destornillador plano	flathead	*flátjed ssscrúdráiver*
desarmador/ destornillador punta de cruz	Phillips	*fílips*
disco de sierra automática	circular saw blade	*sérkiular só bléid*
doblador de varilla	rebar bender	*ríbar bénder*
embudo	funnel	*fánel*
engrapadora	stapler	*ssstéipler*
engrapadora auotomática	stapler gun	*ssstéipler gan*
escalera de mano	ladder	*láder*
escoba	broom	*brúm*
escuadra	square	*ssscuéar*
	framing square	*fréiming ssscuéar*
	carpenter's square	*cárpinters ssscuéar*
fresadora	router	*ráuder*
gafas/lentes de seguridad	safety goggles/ glasses	*séifty góguels/ gláses*
hacha	axe	*áx*
hilo de plomada	plumb line	*plám láin*
lámpara de trabajo	work light	*wérk láit*
linterna	flashlight	*fláshlait*
llana	square trowel	*ssscuéar tráwel*
llave	wrench	*rénch*
	key	*kí*
llave de cadena	chain pipe with wrench	*chéin páip wíd rénch*
llave de correa/ cincho	strap wrench	*ssstráp rénch*
llave de tuercas	crescent wrench	*crésent rénch*
llave pico de ganso	basin wrench	*béisin rénch*
lijadora	sander	*sánder*
lima	file	*fáil*
manguera	hose	*jóus*

marro	sledgehammer	*sssléchjamer*
martillo	hammer	*jámer*
máscara	mask	*másk*
mazo	sledgehammer	*sssléchjamer*
mezcladora	mixer	*míxer*
navaja	utility knife	*iutílity náif*
nivel	level	*lével*
pala	shovel	*shóvel*
paleta de albañil	masons trowel	*méisons tráwel*
pico	pick	*pík*
pincel	brush	*brash*
pinzas	pliers	*pláiers*
prensa	clamp	*clámp*
regla "T"	t square	*tí ssscuéar*
revolvedora	mixer	*míxer*
rodillo	roller	*róuler*
serrucho	saw	*só*
serrucho de mano	handsaw	*jánd só*
sierra	saw	*só*
sierra alternante/ reciprocante	reciprocating saw	*resíproqueiting só*
sierra circular de mesa	table saw	*téibol só*
sierra circular de mano	circular saw	*sérkiular só*
sierra de cadena	chain saw	*chéin só*
sierra de vaivén	jigsaw	*chígso*
sierra para metales	hack saw	*jákso*
sopladora	blower	*blówer*
soplete	soldering torch	*sóldering tórch*
taladro	drill	*dríl*
taladro de mano	brace and bit	*bréis ánd bít*
tijeras para metal	sheet metal shears	*shít métal shíars*
zapapico	pickaxe	*píkax*

Herr.

LOS MESES DEL AÑO
MONTHS
Mánds

enero	January	*chánuari*
febrero	February	*fébruari*
marzo	March	*márch*
abril	April	*éipril*
mayo	May	*méy*
junio	June	*chún*
julio	July	*chulái*
agosto	August	*ógost*
septiembre	September	*septémber*
octubre	October	*octóuber*
noviembre	November	*novémber*
diciembre	December	*dicémber*

LOS DÍAS DE LA SEMANA
DAYS
Déis

lunes	Monday	*mándei*
martes	Tuesday	*tiúsdei*
miércoles	Wednesday	*wénsdei*
jueves	Thursday	*dúrsdei*
viernes	Friday	*fráidei*
sábado	Saturday	*sáterdei*
domingo	Sunday	*sándei*

LOS NÚMEROS
NUMBERS
Námbers

uno	one	*uán*
dos	two	*tú*
tres	three	*drí*
cuatro	four	*fór*
cinco	five	*fáiv*
seis	six	*síx*
siete	seven	*séven*
ocho	eight	*éit*
nueve	nine	*náin*
diez	ten	*tén*
once	eleven	*iléven*
doce	twelve	*tuélv*
trece	thirteen	*dirtín*
catorce	fourteen	*fortín*
quince	fifteen	*fiftín*
dieciséis	sixteen	*sixtín*
diecisiete	seventeen	*seventín*
dieciocho	eighteen	*eitín*
diecinueve	nineteen	*naintín*
veinte	twenty	*tuénti*
veintiuno	twenty-one	*tuénti-uán*
treinta	thirty	*dérti*
cuarenta	forty	*fórti*
cincuenta	fifty	*fífti*
sesenta	sixty	*síxti*
setenta	seventy	*séventi*
ochenta	eighty	*éiti*
noventa	ninety	*náinti*
cien	one hundred	*uán jándred*
doscientos	two hundred	*tú jándred*
quinientos	five hundred	*fáiv jándred*
mil	one thousand	*uán dáusand*

Meses, Días, Números

PREGUNTAS, RESPUESTAS Y AFIRMACIONES BÁSICAS EN EL TRABAJO
BASIC JOB QUESTIONS, ANSWERS AND STATEMENTS
Béisic chób kuéstions, ánsers and ssstéitments

¿Cuántos hombres tiene para ayudarlo/a?
How many men do you have to help you?
¿Jáu méni men du iú jáv tu jélp iú?

Tengo _____ hombres para ayudarme.
I have _____ men to help me.
Ái jáv _____ men tu jélp mi.

¿Cuán grande es su cuadrilla/equipo?
How big is your crew?
¿Jáu big is iór crú?

Mi cuadrilla/equipo tiene _____ hombres.
My crew has ____ men.
Mái crú jas ____ men.

¿Tiene sus propias herramientas?
Do you have your own tools?
¿Dú iú jáv iór óun túls?

¿Cuándo puede comenzar con este trabajo?
When can you start the job?
¿Wén can iú ssstart de chób?

Puedo comenzar este trabajo la semana que viene.
I can begin the job next week.
Ái can bigín de chób next wík.

¿Cuánto le tomará completar este trabajo?
How long will it take you to complete this job?
¿Jáu long wil it téik iú tu complít dis chób?

Tomará un mes/una semana/un día terminar el trabajo.
It will take a month/week/day to do the job.
It wil téik a mónd/wík/déi tu fínish.

¿Puede darme un estimado para hacer otro trabajo?
Can you give me a bid to do another job?
¿Can iú guív mi a bíd tu dú anóder chób?

Podemos darle un estimado para hacer otro trabajo.
We can give you a bid to do another job.
Wi can guív iú a bíd tu dú anóder chób?

¿Puede trabajar mañana?
Can you work tomorrow?
¿Can iú wérk tumórow?

Puedo trabajar todos los días.
I can work everyday.
Ái can wérk evridéi.

¿Cuánto paga este trabajo?
How much does this job pay?
¿Jáu mach das dis chób péi?

Su paga será $_____ la hora.
Your pay is going to be $_____ per hour.
Iór péi is góing tu bi _____ dólars per áuer.

¿Cuándo es el día de pago?
When is pay day?
¿Wén is péi déi?

Le pagaré al final de la semana/del día/del trabajo.
I will pay you at the end of the week/day/job.
Ái wil péi iú at di end ov de wík/déi/chób.

Frases

EN CONVERSACIÓN
CONVERSATIONAL
Converséishonal

¿Cómo está usted hoy/Cómo le va?
How are you today?
¿Jáu ár iú tudéi?

¿Cómo está su familia?
How is your family?
¿Jáu is iór fámili?

Muy bien, gracias.
Very well, thank you.
Véri wel, dánk iú.

Nos vemos mañana.
I will see you tomorrow.
Ái wil sí iú tumórow.

No estaré aquí mañana.
I will not be here tomorrow.
Ái wil not bi jíar tumórow.

¿Pasó un buen fin de semana?
Did you have a good weekend?
¿Did iú jáv a gúd wíkend?

Sí, pasé un muy buen fin de semana.
Yes, I had a very good weekend.
Iés, ái jád a véri gúd wíkend.

Tiene un buen equipo de hombres.
You have a good crew of men.
Iú jáv a gúd crú ov men.

¿Quiere tomar un descanso para almorzar?
Do you want to take a lunch break?
¿Dú iú want tu téik a lánch bréik?

Su trabajo se ve bien.
Your work looks good.
Iór wérk lúks gúd.

¿Voy a la tienda, necesita algo?
I am going to the store, do you need anything?
Ái am góing tu de ssstór, du iú níd éniding?

¿Qué hora es?
What time is it?
¿Wát táim is it?

GENERAL
GENERAL
Chéneral

¿Habla inglés?
Do you speak English?
¿Dú iú ssspík ínglish?

¿Habla español?
Do you speak Spanish?
¿Dú iú ssspík ssspánish?

Sí.
Yes.
Iés.

No.
No.
Nóu.

Por favor.
Please.
Plís.

Gracias.
Thank you.
Dánk iú.

¿Cuál es su nombre/Cómo se llama?
What is your name?
¿Wát is iór néim?

Mi nombre es…/Me llamo…
My name is…
Mái néim is...

¿Tiene referencias?
Do you have references?
¿Dú iú jáv réfrencis?

Sí, tengo referencias.
Yes, I have references.
Iés, ái jáv réfrencis.

No, no tengo referencias.
No, I do not have references.
Nóu, ái dú not jáv réfrencis.

¿Cuál es su número de teléfono?
What is your phone number?
¿Wát is iór fóun námber?

Mi número es _____.
My phone number is_____.
Mái fóun námber is _____.

MISCELÁNEOS
MISCELLANEOUS
Misceláneos

No se permite el uso de drogas.
Drug use is not tolerated.
Drag iús is not toleréitd.

¿Tiene licencia de conducir?
Do you have a driver's license?
¿Dú iú jáv a dráivers láisens?

¿Adónde puedo conseguir una licencia de conducir?
Where can I get a driver's license?
¿Wéar can ái guét a dráivers láisens?

¿Adónde hay un hospital/una clínica?
Where is the hospital/clinic?
¿Wéar is de jóspital/clínic?

Sosténgalo allí mientras lo clavo.
Hold it there while I nail it.
Jóld it déar wáil ái néil it.

Recoja esto.
Pick this up.
Pik dis ap.

Levántelo un poco.
Raise it a little.
Réis it a lítl.

Bájelo un poco.
Lower it a little.
Lówer it a lítl.

Martille esto.
Hammer this.
Jámer dis.

Consiga a alguien que lo ayude.
Get someone to help you.
Guét sámuan tu jélp iú.

¿Adónde…Adónde está…Adónde están…Qué es eso?
Where…Where is…. Where are…. What is that?
¿Wéar... Wéar is ...Wéar ár... Wát is dát?

¡Tenga cuidado!
Be careful!
¡Bi kérful!

Sígame.
Follow me.
Fólow mi.

Empuje.
Push.
Púsh.

Jale.
Pull.
Púl.

¡Cuidado!
Watch out!
¡Wách áut!

Ayúdeme a cargar esto.
Help me carry this.
Jelp mi cárri dis.

Déjeme ayudarle con eso.
Let me help you with that.
Let mi jélp iú wid dát.

La llave estará escondida aquí.
The key will be hidden here.
De kí wil bi jíden jíar.

Por favor cierre la puerta con llave antes de irse.
Please lock the door when you leave.
Plís lok de dór wén iú lív.

El baño portable está allí atrás.
The port-a-pot is out back.
De pórt-a-pót is áut bák.

El basurero está allá.
The dumpster is over there.
De dámpster is óuver déar.

> ## ALBAÑIL – LADRILLO/PIEDRA
> ### MASON – BRICK/STONE
> *Méison - brik/ssstóun*

¿Cuánto hace que trabaja con ladrillo/piedra?
How long have you been working with brick/stone?
¿Jáu long jáv iú bín wérking wid brik/ssstóun?

Hace _____ años que trabajo con ladrillo/piedra.
I have been working with brick/stone for ___ years.

Ái jáv bín wérking wid brik/ssstóun for _____ iérs.

¿Tiene referencias?
Do you have references?
¿Dú iú jáv réfrencis?

Frases

Sí, tengo referencias.
Yes, I have references.
Iés, ái jáv réfrencis.

No, no tengo referencias.
No, I do not have references.
Nóu, ái dú not jáv réfrencis.

¿Me puede dar un presupuesto por este trabajo?
Can you give me an estimate for this job?
¿Can iú guív mi an éstimeit for dis chób?

¿Cuándo puede comenzar con este proyecto?
When can you start this project?
¿Wén can iú ssstárt dis próchekt?

Puedo comenzar este trabajo la semana que viene/en dos semanas.
I can start this job next week/in two weeks.
Ái can ssstárt dis chób next wík/in tú wíks.

¿Cuánto le tomará completar este trabajo?
How long will it take you to complete this job?
¿Jáu long wil it téik iú tu complít dis chób?

Tomará un día/una semana terminarlo.
It will take a day/week to finish.
It wil téik a déi/wík tu fínish.

¿Tiene sus propias herramientas?
Do you have your own tools?
¿Dú iú jáv iór óun túls?

Debemos colocar ladrillo en este lado de la casa.
We need to brick this side of the house.
Wi níd tu brik dis sáid ov de jáus.

Debemos construir una pared de piedra.
We need to build a stone wall.
Wi níd tu bild a ssstóun wól.

Por favor, tráigame más ladrillos/piedras.
Please bring me more brick/stone.
Plís bring mi mór brik/ssstóun.

Debemos nivelar esta pared.
We need to level this wall.
Wi níd tu lével dis wól.

Frases

Debemos mezclar más argamasa.
We need to mix more mortar.
Wi níd tu mix mór mórtar.

Necesitamos un balde de 5 galones.
We need a 5-gallon bucket.
Wi níd a fáiv gálon báket.

Necesitamos agua limpia.
We need clean water.
Wi níd clín wóder.

Debemos limpiar las juntas de lechada.
We need to clean the grout joints.
Wi níd tu clín de gráut chóints.

Tense el hilo por encima para formar una línea recta.
Pull the string across the top for a straight line.
Púl de ssstring acrós de top for a ssstréit láin.

¿Adónde está el nivel?
Where is the level?
¿Wéar is de lével?

¿Adónde está el nivel láser?
Where is the laser level?
¿Wéar is de léiser lével?

¿Adónde está el mortero/argamasa/la mezcla?
Where is the mortar?
¿Wéar is de mórtar?

Mañana entregarán los ladrillos.
The bricks will be delivered tomorrow.
De briks wil bi delíverd tumórow.

Debemos apilar los ladrillos aquí.
We need to stack the bricks here.
Wi níd tu sssták de briks jíar.

Debemos apilar las piedras aquí.
We need to stack the stones here.
Wi níd tu sssták de ssstóuns jíar.

¿Adónde está la paleta?
Where is the trowel?
¿Wéar is de tráwel?

Debemos instalar/levantar una pared aquí.
We need to dry stack a wall here.
Wi níd tu drái sssták a wól jíar.

Necesitamos más andamiaje.
We need more scaffolding.
Wi níd mór ssscáfolding.

¿Adónde está la carretilla?
Where is the wheel-barrow?
¿Wéar is de wíelbarrow?

¿Cuántos ladrillos más se necesitan?
How many more bricks are needed?
¿Jáu méni mór briks ár nídid?

¿Cuántas piedras más se necesitan?
How many more stones are needed?
¿Jáu méni mór ssstóuns ár nídid?

¿Cuántas bolsas más de argamasa/mezcla se necesitan?
How many more bags of mortar will be needed?
¿Jáu méni mór bags ov mórtar wil bi nídid?

Debemos limpiar el argamasa/la mezcla del ladrillo.
We need to clean the mortar off the brick.
Wi níd tu clín de mórtar of de brik.

Debemos obtener una inspección.
We need to get an inspection.
Wi níd tu guét an inspékshon.

Debemos limpiar el área de trabajo a diario.
We need to clean up the job-site daily.
Wi níd tu clín ap de chób-sáit déili.

CARPINTERÍA
FRAMING
Fréiming

¿Cuánto hace que trabaja en carpintería?
How long have you been framing?
¿Jáu long jáv iú bín fréiming?

Hace _____ años que trabajo en carpintería.
I have been framing for ____ years.
Ái jáv bín fréiming for ____ iérs.

¿Tiene referencias?
Do you have references?
¿Dú iú jáv réfrencis?

Sí, tengo referencias.
Yes, I have references.
Iés, ái jáv réfrencis.

No, no tengo referencias.
No, I do not have references.
Nóu, ái dú not jáv réfrencis.

¿Me puede dar un presupuesto por este trabajo?
Can you give me an estimate for this job?
¿Can iú guív mi an éstimeit for dis chób?

¿Cuándo puede comenzar con este proyecto?
When can you start this project?
¿Wén can iú ssstárt dis próchekt?

Puedo comenzar este trabajo la semana que viene/en dos semanas.
I can start this job next week/in two weeks.
Ái can ssstárt dis chób next wík/in tú wíks.

¿Cuánto le tomará completar este trabajo?
How long will it take you to complete this job?
¿Jáu long wil it téik iú tu complít dis chób?

Tomará un día/una semana terminarlo.
It will take a day/week to finish.
It wil téik a déi/wík tu fínish.

¿Tiene sus propias herramientas?
Do you have your own tools?
¿Dú iú jáv iór óun túls?

Necesitamos más madera.
We need more wood.
Wi níd mór wúd.

Necesitamos más clavos.
We need more nails.
Wi níd mór néils.

Debemos construir un armazón/una estructura conforme los planos del arquitecto.
We need to frame this floor according to the architect's plans.
Wi níd tu fréim dis flór acórding tu di árquitects plans.

¿Puede realizar cortes?
Can you cut?
¿Can iú cat?

Debemos arreglar los sofitos.
We need to fix the soffits.
Wi níd tu fix de sófits.

Debemos construir una cubierta/un balcón.
We need to build a deck.
Wi níd tu bíld a dék.

Debemos revestir con tablas con traslapo/solapo la parte trasera del edificio.
We need to lap side the rear of the building.
Wi níd tu lap sáid de ríar ov de bílding.

Debemos darle las terminaciones a la casa una vez finalizado el muro en seco.
We need to trim-out the house after the dry wall is done.
Wi níd tu trím-áut de háus after de dráiwol is dán.

¿Adónde está el martillo?
Where is the hammer?
¿Wéar is de jámer?

¿Adónde están los clavos?
Where are the nails?
¿Wéar ár de néils?

¿Adónde está la cinta de medir?
Where is the measuring tape?
¿Wéar is de mésharing téip?

¿Adónde está el nivel?
Where is the level?
¿Wéar is de lével?

¿Adónde está el nivel láser?
Where is the laser level?
¿Wéar is de léiser lével?

Mañana entregarán los materiales.
The supplies will be delivered tomorrow.
De sapláis wil bi delíverd tumórow.

Debemos apilar la madera allí.
We need to stack the lumber there.
Wi níd tu sstták de lámber déar.

Debemos construir un armazón/una estructura para un techo a cuatro aguas.
We need to frame for a hip roof.
Wi níd tu fréim for a jíp rúf.

Debemos construir un armazón/una estructura para una ventana vertical de buhardilla/un aposento salidizo.
We need to frame for a dormer.
Wi níd tu fréim for a dórmer.

Necesitamos un hastial.
We need a gable.
Wi níd a géibl.

Debemos instalar tejas de madera.
We need to install shake shingles.
Wi níd tu instól shéik shíngls.

Debemos construir un armazón/una estructura para las canaletas.
We need to frame for the gutters.
Wi níd tu fréim for de gáters.

¿Adónde están las tejas de madera?
Where are the shake shingles?
¿Wéar ár de shéik shíngls.?

Necesitamos más andamiaje.
We need more scaffolding.
Wi níd mór ssscáfolding.

Debemos construir un bastidor/marco para una ventana aquí.
We need to frame for a window here.
Wi níd tu fréim for a window jíar.

Debemos colocar las escaleras.
We need to get the stairs in.
Wi níd tu guét de ssstéars in.

¿Cuál es la inclinación del techo?
What is the pitch of the roof?
¿Wát is de pich ov de rúf?

Necesitamos la clavadora automática.
We need the framing nail gun.
Wi níd de fréiming néil gan.

Necesitamos la pistola para clavos enrollados en tiras/pistola de clavos con tambor.
We need the coil nailer.
Wi níd de cóil néiler.

Debemos secar esto mientras llegua el techista.
We need to dry this in until the roofer gets here.
Wi níd tu drái dis in antíl de rúfer guéts jíar.

Debemos instalar las puertas/ventanas.
We need to install doors/windows.
Wi níd tu instól dórs/windows.

Hay que enrasar esa pared.
That wall needs to be furred out.
Dát wól níds tu bi férd áut.

Frases

Debemos colocarle plomería a esto.
We need to plumb this.
Wi níd tu plámb dis.

Necesitamos tablas para caminar.
We need walk boards.
Wi níd wók bórds.

Necesitamos más apoyo aquí.
We need more support here.
Wi níd mór sapórt jíar.

Necesitamos más de 2x4/2x6/2x8/2x10.
We need more 2x4/2x6/2x8/2x10.
Wi níd mór tú bái fór/tú bái síx/tú bái éit/tú bái tén.

Necesitamos una viga especial aquí.
We need a special beam here.
Wi níd a ssspéshal bím jíar.

Debemos obtener una inspección.
We need to get an inspection.
Wi níd tu guét an inspékshon.

Debemos limpiar el área de trabajo a diario.
We need to clean up the job-site daily.
Wi níd tu clín ap de chób-sáit déili.

CALEFACCIÓN Y AIRE ACONDICIONADO
HVAC
Éich-vee-éi-sí

¿Cuánto hace que trabaja con calefacción y aire acondicionado?
How long have you been working with heating and air?
¿Jáu long jáv iú bín wérking wid híting and éar?

Hace _____ años que trabajo con calefacción y aire acondicionado.
I have been working with heating and air for ___ years.
Ái jáv bín wérking wid híting and éar for _____ iérs.

¿Tiene referencias?
Do you have references?
¿Dú iú jáv réfrencis?

Sí, tengo referencias.
Yes, I have references.
Iés, ái jáv réfrencis.

No, no tengo referencias.
No, I do not have references.
Nóu, ái dú not jáv réfrencis.

¿Me puede dar un presupuesto por este trabajo?
Can you give me an estimate for this job?
¿Can iú guív mi an éstimeit for dis chób?

¿Cuándo puede comenzar con este proyecto?
When can you start this project?
¿Wén can iú ssstárt dis próchekt?

Puedo comenzar este trabajo la semana que viene/en dos semanas.
I can start this job next week/in two weeks.
Ái can ssstárt dis chób next wík/in tú wíks.

¿Cuánto le tomará completar este trabajo?
How long will it take you to complete this job?
¿Jáu long wil it téik iú tu complít dis chób?

Tomará un día/una semana terminarlo.
It will take a day/week to finish.
It wil téik a déi/wík tu fínish.

¿Tiene sus propias herramientas?
Do you have your own tools?
¿Dú iú jáv iór óun túls?

Frases

La unidad/el equipo estará lista/o mañana para conexión.
The unit will be ready to hook up tomorrow.
De únit wil bi rédi tu júk ap tumórow.

Necesitamos más planchas de metal.
We need more sheet metal.
Wi níd mór shít métal.

Debemos instalarle el protector contra la lluvia a la unidad/el equipo.
We need to install the rain guard on the unit.
Wi níd tu instól de réin gárd on de únit.

Chequee el interruptor de circuito.
Check the circuit breaker.
Chék de sérkuit bréiker.

Debemos instalar los conductos de aire en la casa.
We need to run the duct work thru the house.
Wi níd tu ran de dáct wérk drú de jáus.

Debemos instalar una bomba de calefacción.
We need to put in a heat pump.
Wi níd tu put in a jít pamp.

Debemos instalar una unidad/un equipo de gas.
We need to put in a gas unit.
Wi níd tu put in a gas iúnit.

Debemos instalar un tubo de ventilación a través de allí.
We need to install a vent pipe thru there.
Wi níd tu instól a vent páip drú déar.

Utilizaremos un conducto flexible en el ático/sótano.
We will use flex duct in the attic/basement.
Wi wil iús flex dáct in di átic/béisment.

Debemos conectar el gas a la cocina.
We need to hook up the stove for gas.
Wi níd tu júk ap de ssstóuv for gas.

Debemos instalar desviadores aquí.
We need to install diverters here.
Wi níd tu instól daivérters jíer.

¿Adónde está el conducto flexible?
Where is the flex duct?
¿Wéar is de flex dáct?

¿Adónde está el termómetro?
Where is the thermometer?
¿Wéar is de dermómeter?

Necesitamos ventiladores en todos los baños.
We need vent fans in all bathrooms.
Wi níd vent fans in all bádrums.

¿Qué tamaño de unidad/equipo de calefacción y aire acondicionado se necesita para esta casa?
How big of an HVAC unit is needed for this house?
¿Jáu big ov an éich-vee-éi-sí iúnit is nídid for dis jáus?

Debemos remover la unidad/el equipo viejo de la casa.
We need to remove the old unit from the house.
Wi níd tu remúv di óuld iúnit from de jáus.

¿Qué tamaño de retorno se necesita?
What size of a return is needed?
¿Wát sáis ov a ritérn is nídid?

¿Cuántas porciones salen de cada unidad/equipo?
How many feeds come off the unit?
¿Jáu méni fíds cám of de iúnit?

Debemos colocar el interruptor de circuito en encendido/apagado.
We need to turn the circuit breaker on/off.
Wi níd tu térn de sérkuit bréiker on/of.

Necesitamos una bandeja recolectora debajo de la unidad/el equipo.
We need an overflow pan under the unit.
Wi níd an óuverflow pan ánder de iúnit.

Debemos aislar y engrapar todos los ductos duros.
We need to insulate and staple all hard ducting.
Wi níd tu ínsuleit and ssstéipl ól jard dácting.

Debemos utilizar desviadores aquí.
We need to use diverters here.
Wi níd tu iús daivérters jíer.

¿Cuál es el período de garantía de la unidad/el equipo?
What is the warranty of the unit?
¿Wát is de wárranti ov de iúnit?

Debemos colocar el termostato aquí.
We need to put the thermostat here.
Wi níd tu put de dérmostat jíer.

Frases

¿Qué tamaño de rejillas se necesitan para el piso?
What size floor grills are needed?
¿Wát sáis flór grils ár nídid?

Debemos obtener una inspección.
We need to get an inspection.
Wi níd tu guét an inspékshon.

Debemos limpiar el área de trabajo a diario.
We need to clean up the job-site daily.
Wi níd tu clín ap de chób-sáit déili.

CONCRETO
CONCRETE
Cónkrit

¿Cuánto hace que trabaja con concreto?
How long have you been working with concrete?
¿Jáu long jáv iú bín wérking wid cónkrit?

Hace _____ años que trabajo con concreto.
I have been working with concrete for ____ years.
Ái jáv bín wérking wid cónkrit for _____ iérs.

¿Tiene referencias?
Do you have references?
¿Dú iú jáv réfrencis?

Sí, tengo referencias.
Yes, I have references.
Iés, ái jáv réfrencis.

No, no tengo referencias.
No, I do not have references.
Nóu, ái dú not jáv réfrencis.

¿Me puede dar un presupuesto por este trabajo?
Can you give me an estimate for this job?
¿Can iú guív mi an éstimeit for dis chób?

¿Cuándo puede comenzar con este proyecto?
When can you start this project?
¿Wén can iú ssstárt dis próchekt?

Puedo comenzar este trabajo la semana que viene/en dos semanas.
I can start this job next week/in two weeks.
Ái can ssstárt dis chób next wík/in tú wíks.

¿Cuánto le tomará completar este trabajo?
How long will it take you to complete this job?
¿Jáu long wil it téik iú tu complít dis chób?

Tomará un día/una semana terminarlo.
It will take a day/week to finish.
It wil téik a déi/wík tu fínish.

¿Tiene sus propias herramientas?
Do you have your own tools?
¿Dú iú jáv iór óun túls?

¿Lloverá?
Is it going to rain?
¿Is it góin tu réin?

Debemos construir encofrados aquí.
We need to build forms here.
Wi níd tu bíld forms jíer.

Vaciaremos el concreto mañana.
We will pour the concrete tomorrow.
Wi wil pór de cónkrit tumórou.

Debemos alisar ese punto en el concreto.
We need to smooth-out that spot in the concrete.
Wi níd tu smúd-áut dát spót in de cónkrit.

Debemos darle a esto una terminación lisa.
We need to make this a smooth finish.
Wi níd tu méik dis a smúd fínish.

Necesitamos un borde recto.
We need a straight edge.
Wi níd a ssstréit éch.

Debemos lavar el concreto a presión.
We need to power wash the concrete.
Wi níd tu páuer wásh de cónkrit.

Debemos apisonar este área.
We need to tamp this area down.
Wi níd tu támp dis éria dáun.

Necesitamos un nivel.
We need a level.
Wi níd a lével.

Debemos nivelar con el nivel láser.
We need to laser level.
Wi níd tu léiser lével.

Debemos cubrir el concreto con plástico.
We need to cover the concrete with plastic.
Wi níd tu cáver de cónkrit wid plástic.

Necesitamos más bolsas de concreto.
We need more bags of concrete.
Wi níd mór bágs ov cónkrit.

Necesitamos más estacas.
We need more stakes.
Wi níd mór ssstéiks.

Necesitamos más madera.
We need more lumber.
Wi níd mór lámber.

Necesitamos más tableros de madera.
We need more plywood.
Wi níd mór pláiwud.

Necesitamos más tela metálica.
We need more wire mesh.
Wi níd mór wáier mesh.

Necesitamos más barras de refuerzo.
We need more rebar.
Wi níd mór ríbar.

Necesitamos más barras de refuerzo y más alambre de anclaje.
We need more rebar saddles and anchoring wire.
Wi níd mór ríbar sádels and ánkoring wáier.

¿Adónde está el rastrillo?
Where is the rake?
¿Wéar is de réik?

¿Adónde está la pala?
Where is the shovel?
¿Wéar is de shóvel?

¿Adónde está el aplanador?
Where is the bull-float?
¿Wéar is de búlflout?

¿Adónde está la tela metálica?
Where is the metal mesh?
¿Wéar is de métal mesh?

¿Adónde está la barra de refuerzo?
Where is the rebar?
¿Wéar is de ríbar?

¿Adónde está la cinta de precaución?
Where is the caution tape?
¿Wéar is de cóshon téip?

¿Adónde está la cota/el punto de referencia?
Where is the bench mark?
¿Wéar is de bench mark?

¿Cuántas yardas de concreto se van a necesitar?
How many yards of concrete will be needed?
¿Uáu méni iárds ov cónkrit wil bi nídid?

Necesitamos el concreto que está reforzado con fibra de vidrio.
We need the fiberglass reinforced concrete.
Wi níd de fáiberglas reinfórsd cónkrit.

El concreto debe ser de 3.000 libras por pulgada cuadrada/5.000 libras por pulgada cuadrada.
The concrete needs to be 3,000 psi/5,000 psi.
De cónkrit níds tu bi drí dáusand pi es ái/fáiv dáusand pi es ái.

El camión entregará _____ yardas de concreto mañana.
The truck will deliver ____ yards of concrete tomorrow.
De trák wil delíver _____ iárds ov cónkrit tumórou.

Avíseme cuando llegue el camión.
Notify me when the truck arrives.
Nótifai mi wén de trák aráivs.

Debemos inspeccionar el cimiento antes de volcar el concreto.
We need to get the footings inspected before we pour the concrete.
Wi níd tu guét de fútings inspékted bifór we pór de cónkrit.

Debemos limpiar el área de trabajo a diario.
We need to clean up the job-site daily.
Wi níd tu clín ap de chób-sáit déili.

DEMOLICIÓN/LIMPIEZA DE OBRA
DEMOLITION/CLEAN-UP
Demolíshon/Clín-ap

Frases

¿Ha realizado anteriormemente trabajo de remoción/demolición?
Have you ever done tear-out/demolition work before?
¿Jáv iú éver dan téar-áut/demolíshon wérk bifór?

Hace _____ años que realizo trabajo de remoción/demolición.
I have been doing tear-out/demolition work for _____ years.
Ái jáv bín dúing téar-áut/demolíshon wérk for _____iérs.

¿Tiene referencias?
Do you have references?
¿Dú iú jáv réfrencis?

Sí, tengo referencias.
Yes, I have references.
Iés, ái jáv réfrencis.

No, no tengo referencias.
No, I do not have references.
Nóu, ái dú not jáv réfrencis.

Frases

¿Me puede dar un presupuesto por este trabajo?
Can you give me an estimate for this job?
¿Can iú guív mi an éstimeit for dis chób?

¿Cuándo puede comenzar con este proyecto?
When can you start this project?
¿Wén can iú ssstárt dis próchekt?

Puedo comenzar este trabajo la semana que viene/en dos semanas.
I can start this job next week/in two weeks.
Ái can ssstárt dis chób next wík/in tú wíks.

¿Cuánto le tomará completar este trabajo?
How long will it take you to complete this job?
¿Jáu long wil it téik iú tu complít dis chób?

Tomará un día/una semana terminarlo.
It will take a day/week to finish.
It wil téik a déi/wík tu fínish.

¿Tiene sus propias herramientas?
Do you have your own tools?
¿Dú iú jáv iór óun túls?

Debemos demoler todas las paredes y cielorrasos marcados con pintura anaranjada.
We need to tear-out all the walls and ceilings marked with orange paint.
Wi níd tu téar-áut ól de wóls and sílings márkd wid órench péint.

Debemos apilar los ladrillos luego de retirarles el cemento viejo.
We need to stack the bricks up after we get the old cement off of them.
Wi níd tu sssták de briks ap áfter wi guét de óuld semént of ov dém.

Debemos apilar todas las rocas.
We need to put all the rocks in one pile.
Wi níd tu put ól de róks in uán páil.

Debemos apilar todos los escombros prolijamente en el basurero.
We need to stack all the debris in the dumpster neatly.
Wi níd tu sssták ól de debrí in de dámpster nítli.

¿Ya está lleno el basurero?
Is the dumpster full yet?
¿Ís de dámpster ful iét?

Avíseme cuando el basurero esté casi lleno.
Let me know when the dumpster is almost full.
Let mi nóu wén de dámpster is ólmoust ful.

Debemos limpiar el jardín.
We need to clean up the yard.
Wi níd tu clín ap de iárd.

Debemos rastrillar el jardín.
We need to rake the yard.
Wi níd tu réik de iárd.

Debemos barrer esto.
We need to sweep this up.
Wi níd tu swíp dis ap.

¿Adónde está el martillo?
Where is the hammer?
¿Wéar is de jámer?

¿Adónde está la escoba?
Where is the broom?
¿Wéar is de brúm?

¿Adónde está la pala?
Where is the shovel?
¿Wéar is de shóvel?

¿Adónde está el marro/mazo?
Where is the sledgehammer?
¿Wéar is de sléchjamer?

Frases

¿Adónde está la pata de cabra/palanca?
Where is the crow-bar?
¿Wéar is de crów-bar?

¿Adónde está la carretilla?
Where is the wheel-barrow?
¿Wéar is de wíelbarrou?

¿Adónde están los guantes?
Where are the gloves?
¿Wéar ár de glavs?

¿Adónde están los lentes de seguridad?
Where are the safety goggles?
¿Wéar ár de séifti góguels?

Debemos barrer los pisos.
We need to sweep the floors.
Wi níd tu swíp de flórs.

Necesitamos otro basurero.
We need another dumpster.
Wi níd anóder dámpster.

Necesitamos más guantes.
We need more gloves.
Wi níd mór glavs.

Debemos taladrar este concreto.
We need to jack-hammer this concrete out.
Wi níd tu jak-jámer dis cónkrit áut.

Debemos utilizar la retroexcavadora para arreglar este jardín.
We need to use the back hoe to fix this yard.
Wi níd tu iús de bak jóu tu fix dis iárd.

Debemos remover esto.
We need to remove this.
Wi níd tu remúv dis.

Debemos dejar esto.
We need to leave this.
Wi níd tu lív dis.

Debemos demoler esto.
We need to tear this out.
Wi níd tu téar dis áut.

Frases

Debemos remover los ladrillos viejos.
We need to remove the old bricks.
Wi níd tu remúv de óuld briks.

Debemos remover el revestimiento viejo.
We need to remove the old siding.
Wi níd tu remúv di óuld sáiding.

Debemos remover esta madera.
We need to remove this wood.
Wi níd tu remúv dis wúd.

Necesitamos _____ hombres para este trabajo.
We need ___ men for this job.
Wi níd _____ men for dis chób.

El baño portable está allí atrás.
The port-a-pot is out back.
De pórt-a-pót is áut bák.

Debemos limpiar el área de trabajo a diario.
We need to clean up the job-site daily.
Wi níd tu clín ap de chób-sáit déili.

MURO EN SECO
DRY WALL
Dráiwol

¿Cuánto hace que trabaja colocando muros en seco?
How long have you been hanging dry wall?
¿Jáu long jáv iú bín jánging dráiwol?

¿Cuánto hace que trabaja en la terminación de muros en seco?
How long have you been finishing dry wall?
¿Jáu long jáv iú bín fínishing dráiwol?

Hace _____ años que trabajo con muros en seco.
I have been working with dry wall for ___ years.
Ái jáv bín wérking wid dráiwol for _____ iérs.

¿Tiene referencias?
Do you have references?
¿Dú iú jáv réfrencis?

Sí, tengo referencias.
Yes, I have references.
Iés, ái jáv réfrencis.

No, no tengo referencias.
No, I do not have references.
Nóu, ái dú not jáv réfrencis.

¿Me puede dar un presupuesto por este trabajo?
Can you give me an estimate for this job?
¿Can iú guív mi an éstimeit for dis chób?

¿Cuándo puede comenzar con este proyecto?
When can you start this project?
¿Wén can iú ssstárt dis próchekt?

Puedo comenzar este trabajo la semana que viene/en dos semanas.
I can start this job next week/in two weeks.
Ái can ssstárt dis chób next wík/in tú wíks.

¿Cuánto le tomará completar este trabajo?
How long will it take you to complete this job?
¿Jáu long wil it téik iú tu complít dis chób?

Tomará un día/una semana terminarlo.
It will take a day/week to finish.
It wil téik a déi/wík tu fínish.

¿Tiene sus propias herramientas?
Do you have your own tools?
¿Dú iú jáv iór óun túls?

Necesitamos más tablas.
We need more boards.
Wi níd mór bórds.

Necesitamos más barro.
We need more mud.
Wi níd mór mad.

Necesitamos más cinta.
We need more tape.
Wi níd mór téip.

Necesitamos más esquineros.
We need more corner bead.
Wi níd mór córner bíd.

Debemos darle a esto una terminación lisa.
We need to finish this to a smooth finish.
Wi níd tu fínish dis tu a smúd fínish.

¿Cuántas tablas va a necesitar?
How many boards will you need?
¿Jáu méni bórds wil iú níd?

¿Adónde está el barro?
Where is the mud?
¿Wéar is de mad?

¿Adónde está la cinta?
Where is the tape?
¿Wéar is de téip?

¿Adónde están las herramientas de terminación?
Where are the finishing tools?
¿Wéar ár de fínishing túls?

Debemos utilizar cinta de tela aquí.
We need to use mesh tape here.
Wi níd tu iús mesh téip jíar.

Debemos colocar el ventilador aquí.
We need to put the fan in here.
Wi níd tu put de fan in jíar.

Necesitamos más andamiaje.
We need more scaffolding.
Wi níd mór ssscáfolding.

¿Cuándo entregarán las tablas?
When will the boards be delivered?
¿Wén wil de bórds bi delíverd?

Debemos apilar las tablas allí.
We need to stack the boards there.
Wi níd tu sssták de bórds déar.

Debemos utilizar tornillos de 2 y de 1 ? pulgadas.
We need to use 2" screws/1 ?" screws.
Wi níd tu iús tú inch ssscrús/uán inch and uán kuárter ssscrús.

Debemos reparar este yeso.
We need to repair this plaster.
Wi níd tu ripéar dis plláster.

Debemos arreglar las rajas/grietas en la pared.
We need to fix the cracks in the wall.
Wi níd tu ripéar de cráks in de wól.

Debemos utilizar cinta de tela para arreglar las rajas/grietas.
We need to use mesh tape for fixing cracks.
Wi níd tu iús mesh téip for fíxing cráks.

Debemos utilizar muro en seco de ? pulgada/de 5/8 de pulgada.
We need to use ?" / 5/8" dry wall.
Wi níd tu iús jáf inch/fáiv éits inch dráiwol.

Debemos colgar primero los cielorrasos.
We need to hang the ceilings first.
Wi níd tu jáng de sílings ferst.

Debemos utilizar el barro de 20 minutos/45 minutos.
We need to use the 20 minute/45 minute mud.
Wi níd tu iús de tuénti mínet/fórti mínet mad.

¿Cuántos esquineros se necesitarán?
How many corner beads will be needed?
¿Jáu méni córner bíds wil bi nídid?

Debemos cubrir este área con cinta.
We need to flat tape this area.
Wi níd tu flat téip dis éria.

Debemos colocar cinta esquinera aquí.
We need to use corner tape here.
Wi níd tu iús córner téip jíar.

Debemos colocar el muro en seco de desecho en el basurero.
We need to put scrap dry wall in the dumpster.
Wi níd tu put ssscráp dráiwol in de dámpster.

Debemos arenar más éste área.
We need to sand this area more.
Wi níd tu sand dis éria mór.

Debemos razar éste área una vez más.
We need to skim this area one more time.
Wi níd tu ssskím dis éria uán mór táim.

Debemos limpiar el área de trabajo a diario.
We need to clean up the job-site daily.
Wi níd tu clín ap de chób-sáit déili.

ELECTRICIDAD
ELECTRICAL
Eléktrikal

¿Cuánto hace que es electricista?
How long have you been an electrician?
¿Jáu long jáv iú bín an electríshan?

Hace _____ años que soy electricista.
I have been an electrician for ____ years.
Ái jáv bín an electríshan for _____ iérs.

¿Tiene referencias?
Do you have references?
¿Dú iú jáv réfrencis?

Sí, tengo referencias.
Yes, I have references.
Iés, ái jáv réfrencis.

No, no tengo referencias.
No, I do not have references.
Nóu, ái dú not jáv réfrencis.

¿Me puede dar un presupuesto por este trabajo?
Can you give me an estimate for this job?
¿Can iú guív mi an éstimeit for dis chób?

¿Cuándo puede comenzar con este proyecto?
When can you start this project?
¿Wén can iú ssstárt dis próchekt?

Puedo comenzar este trabajo la semana que viene/en dos semanas.
I can start this job next week/in two weeks.
Ái can ssstárt dis chób next wík/in tú wíks.

¿Cuánto le tomará completar este trabajo?
How long will it take you to complete this job?
¿Jáu long wil it téik iú tu complít dis chób?

Tomará un día/una semana terminarlo.
It will take a day/week to finish.
It wil téik a déi/wík tu fínish.

¿Tiene sus propias herramientas?
Do you have your own tools?
¿Dú iú jáv iór óun túls?

Debemos hacer las conexiones de tubería y de electricidad a la casa.
We need to rough in the house.
Wí níd tu ráf in de jáus.

Debemos instalar los artefactos de iliminación.
We need to install the light fixtures.
Wi níd tu instól de láit fíxchers.

Debemos instalar luces de tarro en esta habitación.
We need to install can lights in this room.
Wi níd tu instól can lights in dís rúm.

Debemos cablear el lavadero con electricidad de 220 voltios.
We need to wire the laundry room for 220 volts.
Wi níd tu wáier de lóndri rúm for tú jándred tuénti vólts.

Necesitamos 110 voltios aquí.
We need 110 volts here.
Wi níd uán jándred tén vólts jíar.

Necesitamos 220 voltios aquí.
We need 220 volts here.
Wi níd tú jándred tuénti vólts jíar.

Debemos cablear para luces de bajo mesada en la cocina.
We need to wire for under-cabinet lights in the kitchen.
Wi níd tu wáier for ánder-kábinet láits in de kíchen.

¿Llegaron ya los artefactos?
Are the fixtures in yet?
¿Ár de fíxchers in iét?

Debemos colocar esta luz en el dormitorio/baño/la cocina.
We need to put this light in the bedroom/bathroom/kitchen.
Wi níd tu put dís láit in de bédrum/bádrum/kíchen.

Debemos colocar esta araña (de luces) en el comedor/vestíbulo.
We need to put this chandelier in the dining room/foyer.
Wi níd tu put dís shandelíer in de dáining rúm/fóier.

¿Cuántos enchufes/interruptores hay en esa habitación?
How many plugs/switches are in that room?
¿Jáu méni plágs/suíches ár in dát rúm?

Debemos colocarle las tapas a los enchufes y a los interruptores.
We need to put the face-plates on the plugs and switches.
Wi níd tu put de féis-pléits on de plágs and suíches.

Debemos conectar/encender la electricidad.
We need to get the electricity turned on.
Wi níd tu guét di electrísiti térnd on.

Frases

Debemos desconectar/apagar la electricidad.
We need to get the electricity turned off.
Wi níd tu guét di electrísiti térnd of.

Debemos instalar el poste temporario.
We need to get the temporary pole installed.
Wi níd tu guét de témporari póul instóld.

Necesitamos más cable Romax.
We need more Romax.
Wi níd mór róumax.

Necesitamos más conductos/tubos.
We need more conduit.
Wi níd mór kónduit.

Necesitamos el dobla conducto/tubo.
We need the conduit bender.
Wi níd de kónduit bénder.

Necesitamos cables para parlantes en la casa.
We need speaker wires in the house.
Wi níd spíker wáiers in de jáus.

¿Vamos a utilizar cable de fibra óptica en esta casa?
Are we using fiber-optic cable in this house?
¿Ár wi iúsing fáiber-óptic kéibl in dís jáus?

Jale el cable a través de la pared.
Pull the wire thru the wall.
Púl de wáier drú de wól.

¿Adónde está el cortacables?
Where are the wire cutters?
¿Wéar ár de wáier cáders?

¿Adónde está el destornillador/desarmador?
Where is the screwdriver?
¿Wéar is de ssscrúdráiver?

¿Adónde está el martillo?
Where is the hammer?
¿Wéar is de jámer?

¿Adónde está la caja de fusibles?
Where is the fuse box?
¿Wéar is de fiús bóx?

¿Adónde está el dobla conducto/tubo?
Where is the conduit bender?
¿Wéar is de kónduit bénder?

No toque el botón brillante rojo.
Don't touch the shiny red button.
Dóunt tách de sháini red bádon.

Necesitamos TV de cable en los dormitorios.
We need cable T.V. in the bedrooms.
Wi níd kéibl ti ví in de bédrums.

Necesitamos TV de cable en el cuarto de estar.
We need cable T.V. in the den.
Wi níd kéibl ti ví in de dén.

Debemos colocar el ventilador de techo en esta habitación.
We need to put the ceiling fan in this room.
Wi níd tu put de síling fán in dís rúm.

Debemos colocar las luces de tarro primero, aquí en el centro.
We need to put can lights here, center first.
Wi níd tu put can láits jíer, sénter férst.

Necesitamos una caja metálica para dos enchufes/interruptores aquí.
We need a two gang box here.
Wi níd a tú gáng bóx jíer.

Necesitamos una caja metálica para tres enchufes/interruptores aquí.
We need a three gang box here.
Wi níd a drí gáng bóx jíer.

Necesitamos un tres vías desde aquí hasta allí.
We need a three-way from here to here.
Wi níd a drí-wéi from jíer tu jíer.

Debemos obtener una inspección.
We need to get an inspection.
Wi níd tu guét an inspékshon.

Debemos colocar los escombros en el basurero.
We need to put the debris in the dumpster.
Wi níd tu put de debrí in de dámpster.

Debemos limpiar el área de trabajo a diario.
We need to clean up the job-site daily.
Wi níd tu clín ap de chób-sáit déili.

PISOS - MADERA/BALDOZA/ALFOMBRA
FLOORS – WOOD/TILE/CARPET
Flórs – Wúd/Táil/Cárpet

¿Cuánto hace que trabaja colocando pisos?
How long have you been doing floors?
¿Jáu long jáv iú bín dúing flórs?

Hace _____ años que trabajo colocando pisos.
I have been doing floors for ___ years.
Ái jáv bín dúing flórs for _____ iérs.

¿Tiene referencias?
Do you have references?
¿Dú iú jáv réfrencis?

Sí, tengo referencias.
Yes, I have references.
Iés, ái jáv réfrencis.

No, no tengo referencias.
No, I do not have references.
Nóu, ái dú not jáv réfrencis.

¿Me puede dar un presupuesto por este trabajo?
Can you give me an estimate for this job?
¿Can iú guív mi an éstimeit for dis chób?

¿Cuándo puede comenzar con este proyecto?
When can you start this project?
¿Wén can iú ssstárt dis próchekt?

Puedo comenzar este trabajo la semana que viene/en dos semanas.
I can start this job next week/in two weeks.
Ái can ssstárt dis chób next wík/in tú wíks.

¿Cuánto le tomará completar este trabajo?
How long will it take you to complete this job?
¿Jáu long wil it téik iú tu complít dis chób?

Tomará un día/una semana terminarlo.
It will take a day/week to finish.
It wil téik a déi/wík tu fínish.

¿Tiene sus propias herramientas?
Do you have your own tools?
¿Dú iú jáv iór óun túls?

PISOS/MADERA
FLOORS/WOOD
Flórs/Wúd

Debemos colocar este piso.
We need to lay this floor.
Wi níd tu léi dis flór.

Debemos realizar el acabado de los pisos de madera.
We need to refinish the hard wood floors.
Wi níd tu rifínish de járd wúd flórs.

Debemos arenar los pisos.
We need to sand the floors.
Wi níd tu sand de flórs.

Necesitamos tres capas de poliuretano en los pisos.
We need three coats of poly on the floors.
Wi níd drí cóuts ov poli on de flórs.

Queremos los pisos con una terminación satinada.
We want a satin finish on the floors.
Wi want a satin fínish on de flórs.

Necesitamos más papel de lija.
We need more sand paper.
Wi níd mór sand péipar.

Necesitamos el bordeador.
We need the edger.
Wi níd di écher.

Debemos limpiar el piso.
We need to wipe the floor down.
Wi níd tu wáip de flór dáun.

Necesitamos trapos limpios.
We need clean rags.
Wi níd clín rags.

¿Adónde están los protectores de rodillas?
Where are the knee-pads?
¿Wéar ár de ní-pads?

¿Adónde están las máscaras protectoras?
Where are the safety masks?
¿Wéar ár de séifti masks?

Frases

Utilice el bordeador para ir alrededor del perímetro de la habitación.
Use the edger to go around the perimeter of the room.
Iús de écher tu góu aráund de perímeter ov de rúm.

¿Adónde está el aguarrás?
Where are the mineral spirits?
¿Wéar ár de mineral ssspírits?

Una vez que el piso se seque, debemos colocar papel para protegerlo.
We need to put paper down after the floor dries to protect it.
Wi níd tu put péipar dáun after de flór dráis tu protect it.

Mañana podremos caminar sobre los pisos.
We can walk on the floors tomorrow.
Wi can wók on de flórs tumórow.

Debemos limpiar el área de trabajo a diario.
We need to clean up the job-site daily.
Wi níd tu clín ap de chób-sáit déili.

PISOS/BALDOZA
FLOORS/TILE
Flórs/Táil

Debemos instalar baldoza cerámica en el baño/la cocina.

We need to install ceramic tile in the bathroom/kitchen.
Wi níd tu instól cerámic táil in de bádrum/kíchen.

Necesitamos más lechada.
We need more grout.
Wi níd mór gráut.

Necesitamos más baldoza.
We need more tile.
Wi níd mór táil.

Debemos limpiar la lechada.
We need to clean off the grout.
Wi níd tu clín of de gráut.

Necesitamos un balde de 5 galones.
We need a 5-gallon bucket.
Wi níd a fáiv gálon báket.

Necesitamos agua limpia.
We need clean water.
Wi níd clín wóder.

Frases

Necesitamos una esponja limpia.
We need a clean sponge.
Wi níd a clín ssspónch.

Necesitamos el serrucho para baldoza.
We need the tile saw.
Wi níd de táil só.

Necesitamos el molinillo.
We need the grinder.
Wi níd de gráinder.

¿Puede cortar baldoza?
Can you cut tile?
¿Can iú cat táil?

¿Adónde está la lechada?
Where is the grout?
¿Wéar is de gráut?

¿Adónde está la baldoza?
Where is the tile?
¿Wéar is de táil?

¿Adónde está el serrucho?
Where is the saw?
¿Wéar is de só?

Debemos limpiar el área de trabajo a diario.
We need to clean up the job-site daily.
Wi níd tu clín ap de chób-sáit déili.

PISOS/ALFOMBRA
FLOORS/CARPET
Flórs/Cárpet

Debemos tomar medidas para la alfombra.
We need to measure for carpet.
Wi níd tu méshar for cárpet.

La alfombra ya está pedida.
The carpet is on order.
De cárpet is on order.

Debemos colocar primero el bajoalfombra.
We need to install the pad first.
Wi níd tu instól de pad ferst.

Debemos instalar una cartelera/tabla de tachuelas.
We need to install the tack boards.
Wi níd tu instól the tác bórds.

Necesitamos la plancha caliente y la cinta.
We need the hot-iron and tape.
Wi níd de jót-áiron and téip.

Necesitamos el aplanador para alfombra.
We need the carpet stretcher.
Wi níd de cárpet ssstrécher.

Necesitamos cuchillas de navaja afiladas.
We need sharp utility blades.
Wi níd shárp iutílity bléids.

Mañana entregarán la alfombra.
The carpet will be delivered tomorrow.
De cárpet wil bi delíverd tumórow.

Avíseme cuando llegue.
Notify me when it gets here.
Nótifai mi wén it guéts jíar.

Debemos alfombrar la habitación/el closet.
We need to put the carpet in the bedroom/closet.
Wi níd tu put de cárpet in de bédrum/clóset.

Debemos limpiar el área de trabajo a diario.
We need to clean up the job-site daily.
Wi níd tu clín ap de chób-sáit déili.

PINTURA
PAINTING
Péinting

¿Cuánto hace que pinta?
How long have you been painting?
¿Jáu long jáv iú bín péinting?

Hace _____ años que pinto.
I have been painting for ___ years.
Ái jáv bín péinting for ____ iérs.

¿Tiene referencias?
Do you have references?
¿Dú iú jáv réfrencis?

Sí, tengo referencias.
Yes, I have references.
Iés, ái jáv réfrencis.

No, no tengo referencias.
No, I do not have references.
Nóu, ái dú not jáv réfrencis.

¿Me puede dar un presupuesto por este trabajo?
Can you give me an estimate for this job?
¿Can iú guív mi an éstimeit for dis chób?

¿Cuándo puede comenzar con este proyecto?
When can you start this project?
¿Wén can iú ssstárt dis próchekt?

Puedo comenzar este trabajo la semana que viene/en dos semanas.
I can start this job next week/in two weeks.
Ái can ssstárt dis chób next wík/in tú wíks.

¿Cuánto le tomará completar este trabajo?
How long will it take you to complete this job?
¿Jáu long wil it téik iú tu complít dis chób?

Tomará un día/una semana terminarlo.
It will take a day/week to finish.
It wil téik a déi/wík tu fínish.

¿Tiene sus propias herramientas?
Do you have your own tools?
¿Dú iú jáv iór óun túls?

Necesitamos más pintura.
We need more paint.
Wi níd mór péint.

Necesitamos más pinceles.
We need more brushes.
Wi níd mór brashes.

Necesitamos más rodillos.
We need more rollers.
Wi níd mór róulers.

Necesitamos más cinta.
We need more tape.
Wi níd mór téip.

Necesitamos más trapos para limpiar.
We need more drop cloths.
Wi níd mór drop clods.

Debemos colocar la primera capa de pintura en las paredes y en los cielorrasos.
We need to get the first coat of paint on the walls and ceilings.
Wi níd tu guét de ferst cóut ov péint on de wóls and sílings.

Debemos raspar la pintura vieja.
We need to strip the old paint off.
Wi níd tu ssstrip di óuld péint of.

Debemos arenar.
We need to sand.
Wi níd tu sand.

Debemos enmasillar.
We need to caulk.
Wi níd tu cók.

Debemos raspar/rasquetear y realizar el trabajo preparativo.
We need to scrape and do the prep work.
Wi níd tu ssscréip and dú de prep wérk.

Necesitamos una capa de protector y dos capas de base.
We need one coat of primer and two coats of base.
Wi níd uán cóut of práimer and tú cóuts ov béis.

Debemos raspar/rasquetear las ventanas.
We need to scrape the windows.
Wi níd tu ssscréip de wíndows.

¿Adónde está la pintura para esta habitación?
Where is the paint for this room?
¿Wéar is de péint for dis rúm?

Debemos lavar los pinceles.
We need to wash out the brushes.
Wi níd tu wash áut de brashes.

¿Adónde están los pinceles?
Where are the brushes?
¿Wéar ár de brashes?

¿Adónde están los rodillos?
Where are the rollers?
¿Wéar ár de róulers?

¿Adónde está el aguarrás?
Where are the mineral spirits?
¿Wéar ár de míneral ssspírits?

Necesitamos más trapos.
We need more rags.
Wi níd mór rags.

Necesitamos un balde de agua.
We need a bucket of water.
Wi níd a baket ov wóder.

Debemos limpiar los pinceles aquí.
We need to clean brushes over here.
Wi níd tu clín brashes óuver déar.

Necesitamos el poste de extensión.
We need the extension pole.
Wi níd di exténshon póul.

¿Adónde está el poste de extensión.
Where is the extension pole?
¿Wéar is di exténshon póul?

Necesitamos la escalera.
We need the ladder.
Wi níd de láder.

Debemos colocarle a esto una capa de protector antes de instalarlo.
We need to prime this before installing.
Wi níd tu práim dis bifór instóling.

Debemos arenar esto antes de colocar la capa final de pintura.
We need to sand this before the final coat of paint.
Wi níd tu sand dis bifór de fáinal cóut ov péint.

Debemos enmasillar aquí.
We need to caulk here.
Wi níd tu cók jíar.

Debemos retocar aquí.
We need to touch-up here.
Wi níd tu tach-ap jíar.

Debemos pintar la habitación/la cocina/el baño.
We need to paint the bedroom/kitchen/bathroom.
Wi níd tu péint de bédrum/kíchen/bádrum.

Debemos colocar el color principal aquí.
We need to put the body color here.
Wi níd tu put de bodi cólor jíar.

Debemos colocar el color para la madera moldeada aquí.
We need to put the trim color here.
Wi níd tu put de trim cólor jíar.

Debemos colocar el tercer color aquí.
We need to put the 3rd color here.
Wi níd tu put de dérd cólor jíar.

Nos vemos mañana.
I will see you tomorrow.
Ái wil sí iú tumórow.

Debemos limpiar el área de trabajo a diario.
We need to clean up the job-site daily.
Wi níd tu clín ap de chób-sáit déili.

PLOMERÍA
PLUMBING
Pláming

¿Cuánto hace que es plomero?
How long have you been a plumber?
¿Jáu long jáv iú bín a plámer?

Hace _____ años que soy plomero.
I have been a plumber for ___ years.
Ái jáv bín a plámer for _____ iérs.

¿Tiene referencias?
Do you have references?
¿Dú iú jáv réfrencis?

Sí, tengo referencias.
Yes, I have references.
Iés, ái jáv réfrencis.

No, no tengo referencias.
No, I do not have references.
Nóu, ái dú not jáv réfrencis.

¿Me puede dar un presupuesto por este trabajo?
Can you give me an estimate for this job?
¿Can iú guív mi an éstimeit for dis chób?

¿Cuándo puede comenzar con este proyecto?
When can you start this project?
¿Wén can iú ssstárt dis próchekt?

Puedo comenzar este trabajo la semana que viene/en dos semanas.
I can start this job next week/in two weeks.
Ái can ssstárt dis chób next wík/in tú wíks.

¿Cuánto le tomará completar este trabajo?
How long will it take you to complete this job?
¿Jáu long wil it téik iú tu complít dis chób?

Tomará un día/una semana terminarlo.
It will take a day/week to finish.
It wil téik a déi/wík tu fínish.

¿Tiene sus propias herramientas?
Do you have your own tools?
¿Dú iú jáv iór óun túls?

Debemos conectar el agua.
We need to get the water turned on.
Wi níd tu guét de wóder térnd on.

Debemos desconectar el agua.
We need to get the water turned off.
Wi níd tu guét de wóder térnd of.

Debemos hacer las conexiones de tubería y de electricidad a la casa.
We need to rough in the house.
Wi níd tu ráf in de jáus.

Debemos arreglar la obstrucción.
We need to fix the clog.
Wi níd tu fix de clog.

¿Cuántos grifos habrá en la casa?
How many faucets will there be in the house?
¿Jáu méni fósets wil déar bi in de jáus?

¿Ya llegaron los artefactos?
Are the fixtures in yet?
¿Ár de fíxchers in iét?

Necesitamos más cañería de cobre.
We need more copper pipe.
Wi níd mór cóper páip.

frases

Necesitamos más cañería de plástico.
We need more PVC pipe.
Wi níd mór pee-vee-sí páip.

Debemos colocar este grifo en la cocina/el baño/la lavandería.
We need to put this faucet in the kitchen/bathroom/laundry room.
Wi níd tu put dis fóset in de kíchen/bádrum/lóndri rúm.

Debemos excavar una nueva canaleta en el jardín del frente.
We need to dig a new water line in the front yard.
Wi níd tu dig a niú wóder láin in de front iárd.

Debemos sopletear ese caño.
We need to solder that pipe.
Wi níd tu sólder dat páip.

¿Ha encontrado la pérdida?
Have you found the leak?
¿Jáv iú fáund de lík?

¿Ha encontrado la llave de tubo.
Where is the pipe-wrench?
¿Wéar is de páip-rénch?

¿Adónde está la pala?
Where is the shovel?
¿Wéar is de shóvel?

¿Adónde está el martillo?
Where is the hammer?
¿Wéar is de jámer?

¿Adónde está el antorcha de propano?
Where is the propane torch?
¿Wéar is de propéin torch?

¿Adónde está el pegamento?
Where is the glue?
¿Wéar is de glú?

¿Adónde está el pozo séptico?
Where is the septic system?
¿Wéar is de séptic sístem?

¿Adónde está la bomba?
Where is the pump?
¿Wéar is de pámp?

Frases

Debemos desconectar el agua de la calle.
We need to turn the water off at the street.
Wi níd tu térn de wóder of at de ssstrít.

Debemos colocar una bandeja de desagüe/drenaje aquí.
We need to put a drain pan here.
Wi níd tu put a dréin pan jíer.

Debemos retirar esta cañería.
We need to pull this piping out.
Wi níd tu púl dis páiping áut.

Debemos obtener una inspección.
We need to get an inspection.
Wi níd tu guét an inspékshon.

Debemos limpiar el área de trabajo a diario.
We need to clean up the job-site daily.
Wi níd tu clín ap de chób-sáit déili.

TECHADO
ROOFING
Rúfing

¿Cuánto hace que es techista?
How long have you been roofing?
¿Jáu long jáv iú bín rúfing?

Hace _____ años que soy techista.
I have been roofing for ___ years.
Ái jáv bín rúfing for ___ iérs.

¿Tiene referencias?
Do you have references?
¿Dú iú jáv réfrencis?

Sí, tengo referencias.
Yes, I have references.
Iés, ái jáv réfrencis.

No, no tengo referencias.
No, I do not have references.
Nóu, ái dú not jáv réfrencis.

¿Me puede dar un presupuesto por este trabajo?
Can you give me an estimate for this job?
¿Can iú guív mi an éstimeit for dis chób?

Frases

¿Cuándo puede comenzar con este proyecto?
When can you start this project?
¿Wén can iú ssstárt dis próchekt?

Puedo comenzar este trabajo la semana que viene/en dos semanas.
I can start this job next week/in two weeks.
Ái can ssstárt dis chób next wík/in tú wíks.

¿Cuánto le tomará completar este trabajo?
How long will it take you to complete this job?
¿Jáu long wil it téik iú tu complít dis chób?

Tomará un día/una semana terminarlo.
It will take a day/week to finish.
It wil téik a déi/wík tu fínish.

¿Tiene sus propias herramientas?
Do you have your own tools?
¿Dú iú jáv iór óun túls?

Debemos arrancar y desechar el techo viejo.
We need to tear-off and dispose of the old roof.
Wi níd tu téar-of and dispóus ov di óuld rúf.

Necesitamos un basurero.
We need a dumpster.
Wi níd a dámpster.

Necesitamos más tejas.
We need more shingles.
Wi níd mór shínguels.

Necesitamos más fieltro.
We need more felt.
Wi níd mór félt.

Necesitamos más clavos.
We need more nails.
Wi níd mór néils.

Necesitamos más andamiaje.
We need scaffolding.
Wi níd ssscáfolding.

Debemos colocar cubrejuntas alrededor de la chimenea.
We need to flash around the chimney.
Wi níd tu flash aráund de chímni.

¿Adónde están las tejas?
Where are the shingles?
¿Wéar ár de shínguels?

¿Adónde está el fieltro?
Where is the felt?
¿Wéar is de félt?

¿Adónde están los clavos?
Where are the nails?
¿Wéar ár de néils?

¿Adónde está el martillo?
Where is the hammer?
¿Wéar is de jámer?

¿Adónde está el serrucho?
Where is the saw?
¿Wéar is de só?

¿Adónde están las tenazas para techar?
Where is the roofing fork?
¿Wéar is de rúfing fork?

¿Adónde está el pistola para clavos enrollados en tiras/pistola de clavos de tambor?
Where is the coil nailer?
¿Wéar is de cóil néiler?

Mañana entregarán las tejas.
The shingles will be delivered tomorrow.
De shínguels wil bi delíverd tumórow.

Avíseme cuando lleguen las tejas.
Notify me when the shingles arrive.
Nótifai mi wén de shínguels arráiv.

Debemos utilizar tejas de madera/ripias en el techo.
We need to use shake shingles on this roof.
Wi níd tu iús shéik shínguels on dis rúf.

Debemos utilizar tejas arquitectónicas de 30 años de durabilidad en éste techo.
We need to use 30-yr, architectural shingles on this roof.
Wi níd tu iús dérti-iér, arquitékchural shínguels on dis rúf.

Debemos utilizar tejas/pizarras en este techo.
We need to use slate on this roof.
Wi níd tu iús sssléit on dis rúf.

Frases

Debemos utilizar metal en este techo.
We need to use metal on this roof.
Wi níd tu iús métal on dis rúf.

Debemos utilizar un canal de ventilación aquí.
We need to use ridge-venting here.
Wi níd tu iús rídch-vénting jíar.

Debemos utilizar caucho aquí.
We need to use rubber here.
Wi níd tu iús raber jíar.

¿Cuál es la inclinación del techo?
What is the pitch of the roof?
¿Wát is de pich ov de rúf?

Debemos colocar tragaluces/claraboyas aquí.
We need to put skylights here.
Wi níd tu put ssskáilaits jíer.

Debemos colocar cubrejuntas alrededor de los tragaluces/las claraboyas.
We need to flash around the skylights.
Wi níd tu flash aráund de ssskáilaits.

¿Sabe cómo trabajar con techos de metal?
Can you do metal roofs?
¿Can iú dú métal rúfs?

¿Sabe cómo trabajar con techos de cobre?
Can you do copper roofs?
¿Can iú dú cóper rúfs?

Debemos reemplazar la cubierta/el balcón aquí.
We need to replace the decking here.
Wi níd tu ripléis de déking jíer.

Necesitamos una cubierta nueva/un balcón nuevo aquí.
We need new decking.
Wi níd niú déking.

Debemos colocarle cubrejuntas de cobre a la chimenea.
We need to flash the chimney in copper.
Wi níd tu flash de chímni in cóper.

Debemos utilizar techo de caucho.
We need to use rubber roofing.
Wi níd tu iús raber rúfing.

Debemos pegar/adherir el techo.
We need to glue the roof down.
Wi níd tu glú de rúf dáun.

Debemos utilizar un canalete de desagüe.
We need to use drip edge.
Wi níd tu iús drip éch.

Debemos colocarle cubrejuntas a esto.
We need to flash this.
Wi níd tu flash dis.

Debemos instalar ventilaciones de techo aquí.
We need to install roof vents here.
Wi níd tu instól rúf vents jíer.

Debemos utilizar un canal de ventilación.
We need to use ridge vent on the house.
Wi níd tu iús rídch vent on de jáus.

Debemos primero arrancar las tejas.
We need to tear-off shingles first.
Wi níd tu téar-of shínguels ferst.

Debemos utilizar una lona para atajar las tejas.
We need to use a tarp to catch shingles.
Wi níd tu iús a tarp tu cach shínguels.

Debemos colocar las tejas y los escombros en el basurero.
We need to put shingles and debris in the dumpster.
Wi níd tu put shínguels and debrí in de dámpster.

Debemos enmasillar aquí.
We need to caulk here.
Wi níd tu cók jíer.

Debemos obtener una inspección.
We need to get an inspection.
Wi níd tu guét an inspékshon.

Debemos limpiar el área de trabajo a diario.
We need to clean up the job-site daily.
Wi níd tu clín ap de chób-sáit déili.

Frases

La Lingo Guide Para Constructores
Suplemento sobre seguridad

¡La seguridad es prioridad!
Safety is Priority!
¡Séifti is praióriti!

La información de esta sección proviene de material de OSHA.
Information for this section came from OSHA material.
Informéishon for dís sécshon kéim from OSHA matírial.

Para mayor información,
por favor contacte a:
info@thelingoguide.com
www.thelingoguide.com

Published by:
The Lingo Guide, LLC
Nashville, TN

Esta publicación no podrá ser reproducida, guardada o archivada en ningún sistema de computación ni transmitida en forma parcial o completa, ya sea por métodos electrónicos o mecánicos, por fotocopias, por medio de grabación o por cualquier otro método, sin la previa autorización de The Lingo Guide, LLC.
Copyright ©2006 The Lingo Guide, LLC. All rights reserved. v1.1

Índice

El propósito de "The Lingo Guide para Constructores" es el de servir
exclusivamente como una herramienta para facilitar la comunicación entre gente
de habla inglesa y gente de habla hispana. La finalidad de esta guía no es para
que sea utilizada en ningún tipo de comunicado legal. El editor, publicador y el
autor no se responsabilizan por los errores, omisiones o daños que pudiere causar
el uso de la información contenida en "The Lingo Guide para Constructores".

A

acero	steel	*ssstíl*
aire comprimido	compressed air	*comprésd éar*
amarra, ligadura	tie-off	*tái óff*
ambulancia	ambulance	*ámbiulans*
andamiaje	scaffolding	*ssscáfolding*
andamiaje de caño	pole scaffold	*póul ssscáfold*
andamiaje de doble caño	double pole scaffold	*dábl póul ssscáfold*
andamiaje móvil	mobile scaffold	*móubail ssscáfold*
andamio de caballete/ de burros	horse scaffold	*jórs ssscáfold*
antideslizante	slip resistant	*ssslíp resístant*
apuntalamiento, equipo de soporte	shoring	*shóring*
área de almacenaje	storage area	*ssstórech éria*
área de uso obligatorio de casco	hard hat area	*járd ját éria*
arnés	harness	*járnes*
arnés de seguridad	safety harness	*séifti járnes*
ayuda	help	*jélp*

B

balance	balance	*bálans*
balón	ball	*ból*
barra/riel superior	top rail	*tóp réil*
barrera de seguridad	guardrail	*gárdreil*
barricada	barricade	*barrikéid*
batería	battery	*báteri*
bola de demolición	wrecking ball	*réking ból*
bota/calzado de trabajo	work boot	*uérk bút*
botiquín de primeros auxilios	first aid kit	*férst éid kít*

C

cable detonador	detonating cord	*detonéiting córd*
cabría	derrick	*dérrik*
caída	fall	*fól*
caja de trinchera, mula	trench box	*trénch bóx*
camión	truck	*trák*
camión de cemento	cement truck	*semént trák*
capacidad	capacity	*capáciti*
capacidad de carga	load capacity	*lóud capáciti*

carga calculada	rated load	*réited lóud*
cargador	loader	*lóuder*
cargador de baterías	battery charger	*báteri chárcher*
cartel de peligro	danger/hazard sign	*déincher/jásard sáin*
cartel para prevención de accidentes	accident prevention sign	*áccident prevénshon sáin*
casco	hard hat	*járd ját*
cascos protectores/ de seguridad	protective helmets	*protéctiv jélmets*
cinturón de seguridad	safety belt	*séifti bélt*
clase sobre seguridad	safety class	*séifti clás*
clasificación del suelo	soil classification	*sóil clasifikéichon*
clínica	clinic	*clínic*
combustible	combustible	*combástibl*
comunicación sobre peligros	hazard communication	*jázard comiunikéishon*
conducto	pipeline	*páiplain*
conducto, canaleta	chutes	*shúts*
contrapeso	counter weight	*cáunter wéit*
contrato sobre seguridad	safety contract	*séifti kóntract*
cordón	lanyard	*lániard*
croquis/diseño de obra/ del sitio	site layout	*sáit léiaut*
cubierta pre-fabricada	fabricated deck	*fabrikéitd dék*
cuerda de soporte	suspension rope	*saspénshon róup*
cuerda salvavidas, cerca de seguridad	life line	*láif láin*

D

demostrar	demonstrate	*démonstreit*
derrumbe, socavado, desprendimiento	cave-in	*kéiv in*
destrucción (con explosivos)	blasting	*blásting*

E

eléctrico	electric	*eléctric*
elevador	elevator	*elevéitor*
elevador aéreo	aerial lift	*áirial líft*
elevando y apuntalando	hoisting and rigging	*hóisting ánd ríging*
entablillar	splint	*sssplínt*
entrenamiento contínuo	on-going training	*óngoing tréining*
entrenamiento sobre seguridad	safety training	*séifti tréining*

equipamiento para protección personal	personal protective equipment	*pérsonal protéctiv ekuípment*
escalera	stairway	*ssstéarwei*
escalera móvil/de mano	ladder	*láder*
espátula	scraper	*ssscréiper*
estampida	boom	*búm*
excavador/a	excavator	*excavéitor*
excavadora	dozer	*dóuser*
explosivo	explosive	*explóusiv*
exposición al ruido	noise exposure	*nóis expóushor*

F

falla	misfire	*misfáier*
fatalidad, muerte	fatality	*fatálity*
flotar, elemento de flotación	float	*flóut*
fuego	fire	*fáier*
fusible de seguridad	safety fuse	*séifti fiús*

G

gafas de seguridad	safety glasses	*séifti glásis*
gafas protectoras/ de seguridad	protection goggles	*protékshon gógls*
gancho, colgadero	hanger	*jánger*
gato	jack	*chák*
grúa	crane	*créin*
guantes	gloves	*glávs*

H

hidráulico	hydraulic	*jaidrólik*
historia clínica	medical record	*médical récord*
hospital	hospital	*jóspital*
hoyo, pozo	pit	*pít*

I

iluminación	illumination	*iluminéishon*
iluminación	lighting	*láiting*
inflamable	flammable	*flámabl*
inspección de seguridad	safety inspection	*séifti inspékshon*

L

larguero	runner	*ráner*
láteral	lateral side rail	*lateral sáid réil*
levantar, alzar	hoist	*jóist*
libre de accidentes	accident free	*áccident frí*
limpia ojos	eye flush	*ái flásh*

línea de alcantarilla	sewer line	*súer láin*
línea de carga	load line	*lóud láin*
listón, peldaño	cleat	*clít*

M

mantenimiento	maintenance	*méintenans*
marcos protectores/ de seguridad	protective frames	*protéctiv fréims*
máscara protectora	dust mask	*dást másk*
montacargas	forklift	*fórklift*

N

| nivelador, tractor | bulldozer | *búldouser* |
| niveladora | grader | *gréider* |

O

| objetos voladores | flying objects | *fláing óbjects* |
| obstrucción/bloqueo en el agüjero | hole obstruction | *jóul obstrákshon* |

P

palanca	lever	*léver*
paramédico	paramedic	*paramédic*
pasillo	walkway	*wólkwei*
peligro	hazard	*jásard*
peligro de caída	falling hazard	*fóling jásard*
peligro de tropiezo	tripping hazard	*tríping jásard*
pendiente, inclinación, cuesta	slope	*ssslóup*
persona calificada	qualified person	*cualifáid pérson*
persona de contacto en caso de emergencia	emergency contact person	*emérshensi cóntact pérson*
pilote	stilt	*ssstílt*
placas antideslizantes	skid plates	*ssskíd pléits*
plan de acción	action plan	*ákshon plán*
plan de seguridad	safety plan	*séifti plán*
plataforma	platform	*plátform*
polvo	dust	*dást*
portador	conveyor	*konvéior*
poster sobre seguridad	safety poster	*séifti póster*
prevención contra incendio	fire prevention	*fáier prevénshon*
prevención para caídas	fall prevention	*fól prevénshon*
problema eléctrico	electrical problem	*eléktrical próblem*

protección	protection	*protékshon*
protección de enrolle	roll over protection	*róul óuver protékshon*
protección para caídas	fall protection	*fól protékshon*
protección para el rostro	face protection	*féis protékshon*
protección para incendio	fire protection	*fáier protékshon*
protección para la respiración	respiratory protection	*respíratori protékshon*
protección para la cabeza	head protection	*jéd protékshon*
protección para los ojos	eye protection	*ái protékshon*
protección para los oídos	hearing protection	*jíaring protékshon*
puente	bridge	*brích*

R

red de seguridad	safety net	*séifti nét*
refuerzo	bracing	*bréising*
refuerzo en diagonal	diagonal bracing	*daiágonal bréising*
refuerzo en cruz	cross bracing	*crós bréising*
refuerzo horizontal	horizontal bracing	*jorisóntal bréising*
reportar, informar	reporting	*repórting*
retroexcavadora	backhoe	*bákjou*
rodilleras antideslizantes	skid pads	*ssskíd páds*
rueda	wheel	*uíel*
ruido	noise	*nóis*

S

salida	means of egress	*míns óv egrés*
salida de escape	means of escape	*míns óv eskéip*
sanidad	sanitation	*sanitéishon*
señalización	signaling	*sígnaling*
servicio médico	medical service	*médical sérvis*
sistema de asistencia a compañeros/	buddy system	*bádi sístem*
sistema de barreras de seguridad	guardrail system	*gárdreil sístem*
soga de alambre	wire rope	*wáier róup*
soga, cuerda	rope	*róup*
soporte de carga	load bearing	*lóud béaring*
soporte, almojaya	bearer	*béarar*
supervisión contínua	on-going supervision	*óngoing supervíshon*
supervisor de seguridad	safety supervisor	*séifti supervísor*

T-Z

tablón de andamiaje	scaffold plank	*ssscáfold plánk*
taladro	jack hammer	*chák jámer*
tapones de oídos	ear plugs	*íar plágs*
traba para la ventana	window jack	*wíndou cháck*
tractor de cadena/ oruga	crawl tractor	*cról tráktor*
vapor	vapor	*véipor*
venda	bandage	*bándech*
ventilación	ventilation	*ventiléishon*
viga	beam	*bím*
viga voladiza, estabilizadores	out-rigger beam	*áut ríguer bím*
violación a la protección para caídas	fall protection violation	*fól protékshon vaioléishon*
zanja	trench	*trénch*

Peligros/Hazards

PELIGROS
HAZARDS
Jásards

caídas	falls	*fóls*
derrumbe de zanja	trench collapse	*trénch coláps*
derrumbe de andamiaje	scaffold collapse	*ssscáfold coláps*
shock eléctrico y arc flash/arc blast	electric shock and arc flash/arc blast	*eléctric shóck ánd árc flash or blast*
falla en el uso correcto del equipamiento protección personal	failure to use proper personal protective equipment	*féiliur tu íus próper pésonal protéctiv ekuípment*

Los 10 aspectos básicos de OSHA

LOS 10 ASPECTOS BÁSICOS DE OSHA
TOP 10 OSHA ISSUES
lohs dee-EHZ ahs-PEHK-tohs BAH-see-kohs deh UH-shah

1. Andamiaje
   Scaffolding
   ssscáfolding

2. Protección para caídas (alcance, aplicación, definiciones)
   Fall Protection (scope, application, definitions)
   fól protécshon (ssscóup, aplikéishon, definíshons)

3. Excavaciones (requisitos generales)
   Excavations (general requirements)
   Exkavéishons (chéneral rekuáierments)

4. Escaleras (móviles/de mano)
   Ladders
   Láders

5. Protección para la cabeza
   Head Protection
   Jéd protécshon

6. **Excavaciones (requisitos para sistemas de protección)**
   Excavations (requirements for protective systems)
   Exkavéishons (rekuáierments for protéktiv sístems)

7. **Comunicaciones sobre peligros**
   Hazard Communication
   Jásard comiunikéishon

8. **Protección de caídas (requisitos para entrenamiento)**
   Fall Protection (training requirements)
   Fól protékshon (tréining rekuáierments)

9. **Construcción (provisiones de seguridad general y de salud)**
   Construction (general safety and health provisions)
   Konstrácshon (chéneral séifti and jéld províshons)

10. **Electricidad (métodos de cableado, de diseño y protección)**
    Electrical (wiring methods, design and protection)
    Eléctrical (uáiaring médods, disáin ánd protéshon)

Frases-Basicas

FRÉISIS-BASICAS
FRASES
FRAH-sehs

¡La seguridad es prioridad!
Safety is priority!
¡Séifti is praióriti!

¡Ande con cuidado!
Be safe!
¡Bí séif!

Tenemos clases periódicas de entrenamiento.
We have regular training classes.
Wí jáv réguiular tréining clásis.

Tenemos entrenamiento periódico sobre seguridad.
We have regular safety training.
Wí jáv réguiular séifti tréining.

Tenemos inspecciones periódicas sobre seguridad.
We have regular safety inspections.
Wí jáv réguiular séifti inspécshons.

Necesitamos una clase sobre seguridad.
We need a safety class.
Wí níd a séifti clás.

Necesitamos una clase de entrenamiento.
We need a training class.
Wí níd a tréining clás.

Utilizamos el sistema de asistencia a los compañeros/colegas.
We use the buddy system.
Wí iús de bádi sístem.

Esta es un área de uso obligatorio de casco.
This is a hard hat area.
Dís is a járd ját éria.

Esta es una zona de destrucción (con explosivos).
This is a blasting zone.
Dís is a blásting sóun.

Todos los botones de emergencia son de color rojo.
All emergency stop buttons are colored red.
Ól emérshensi stóp bátons ár cólord réd.

Debemos limpiar el área de trabajo a diario.
We need to cleanup the job-site daily.
Wí níd tu clínap de chób-sáit déili.

Tenemos un extinguidor para fuegos.
We have a fire extinguisher.
Wí jáv a fáier extíngüisher.

Tenga cuidado.
Be careful.
Bí kérful.

¡Cuidado!
Watch out!
¡Wách áut!

¡Ayúdeme!
Help me!
¡Jélp mi!

No se permiten drogas en este lugar de trabajo.
This is a drug free work-site.
Dís is a drág frí wérk-sáit.

GRÚAS
CRANES
Kréins

Necesitamos una clase sobre seguridad para grúas.
We need a safety class on cranes.
Wí níd a séifti clás on kréins.

Necesitamos realizar un chequeo de seguridad del equipamiento.
We need a safety check on the equipment.
Wí níd a séifti chék on de ecuípment.

Debemos chequear el diagrama de carga.
We need to check the load chart.
Wí níd to chék de lóud chárt.

Debemos delimitar éste área por seguridad.
We need to mark off this area for safety.
Wí níd to márk of dís éria for séifti.

Debemos cerrar este área con barricadas.
We need to barricade this area.
Wí níd tu barrikéid dís éria.

Debemos chequear la cuerda de alambre.
We need to check the wire rope.
Wí níd tu chék de wáier róup.

Debemos chequear las cadenas.
We need to check the chains.
Wí níd tu chék de chéins.

Debemos chequear el gancho.
We need to check the hook.
Wí níd tu chék de júk.

Debemos tener cuidado con los cables eléctricos.
We need to watch out for electric lines.
Wí níd tu wách áut for eléctric láins.

No podemos envolver la carga con las sogas.
We cannot wrap the ropes around the load.
Wí canót ráp de róups aráund de lóud.

No podemos mover la carga por encima de la gente.
We cannot move the load over people.
Wí canót múv de lóud óuver pípol.

SEGURIDAD SOBRE ELECTRICIDAD
ELECTRICAL SAFETY
Eléctrical séifti

Necesitamos una clase de entrenamiento de seguridad sobre electricidad.
We need a training class on electrical safety.
Wí níd a tréining clás on eléctrical séifti.

Necesitamos chequear la seguridad de todos los cables.
We need a safety check on all cords.
Wí níd a séifti chék on ól córds.

Debemos reemplazar este cable que está dañado.
We need to replace this damaged cord.
Wí níd tu ripléis dís dámechd córd.

Debemos reemplazar este cable que está desgastado/pelado.
We need to replace this frayed cord.
Wí níd tu ripléis dís fréid córd.

Debemos localizar los cables de electricidad antes de comenzar a cavar.
We need to locate the electrical lines before digging.
Wí níd tu lokéit di eléctrical láins bifór díging.

Debemos instalar las placas de los interruptores.
We need to install the plates on the switches.
Wí níd tu instól de pléits on de suíches.

PROTECCIÓN DE CAÍDAS
FALL PROTECTION
Fól protécshon

Necesitamos una clase de entrenamiento sobre protección para caídas.
We need a training class on fall protection.
Wí níd a tréining clás on fól protécshon.

Debemos trabajar utilizando las alzadas/los levantamientos.
We need to use the lifts to work on.
Wí níd tu iús de lífts tu wérk on.

Debemos colocar las barreras de protección.
We need to put up the guardrails.
Wí níd tu put áp de gárdreils.

Necesitamos líneas de alerta.
We need warning lines.
Wí níd wórning láins.

Debemos colocar señalización de cuidado.
We need to post warning signs.
Wí níd tu póust wórning sáins.

Debemos tapar los agüjeros del suelo.
We need to cover floor holes.
Wí níd tu cáver flór jóuls.

Debemos utilizar redes de seguridad.
We need to use safety nets.
Wí níd tu iús séifti néts.

Debemos utilizar nuestro arnés de seguridad.
We need to use our safety harness.
Wí níd tu iús áuer séifti járnes.

Necesitamos otro arnés de seguridad.
We need another safety harness.
Wí níd anóder séifti járnes.

¿Adónde están los arnéses de seguridad?
Where are the safety harnesses?
¿Wéar ár de séifti járneses?

Debemos utilizar nuestros cascos.
We need to wear our hard hats.
Wí níd tu wéar áuer járd játs.

PRIMEROS AUXILIOS
FIRST AID
Férst éid

Necesitamos una clase de entrenamiento sobre primeros auxilios.
We need a training class on first aid.
Wí níd a tréining clás on férst éid.

Necesitamos una clase para CPR (resucitación cardio-pulmonar).
We need a training class for CPR.
Wí níd a tréining clás for sí pí ár.

Anunciamos (en lugares públicos) números de emergencia.
We post emergency numbers.
Wí póust emérshensi námbers.

¿Adónde está el hospital?
Where is the hospital?
¿Wéar is de jóspital?

Tenemos un botiquín de primeros auxilios.
We have a first aid kit.
Wí jáv a férst éid kit.

Necesitamos vendas.
We need bandages.
Wí níd bándashes.

¿Está herido/a?
Are you hurt?
¿Ár iú jért?

¿Tiene a alguien a quien contactar?
Do you have someone to contact?
¿Dú iú jáv sámuan tu cóntact?

¿Necesita ver a un doctor?
Do you need to see a doctor?
¿Dú iú níd tu sí a dóctor?

Ya llega asistencia médica para Ud.
Medical help is coming to you.
Médical jélp is cáming tu iú.

¿Se ha vacunado contra el tétano?
Have you had a tetanus shot?
¿Jáv iú jád a tétanus shot?

Ya llega asistencia/ayuda.
Help is on the way.
Jélp is on de wéi.

MONTACARGAS
FORKLIFTS
Fórklifts

Necesitamos una clase de seguridad para montacargas.
We need a safety class on forklifts.
Wí níd a séifti clás on fórklifts.

Necesitamos chequear la seguridad del montacargas antes de utilizarlo.
We need a safety check on the forklift before using.
Wí níd a séifti chék on de fórklift bifór iúsing.

Necesitamos chequear la seguridad de los frenos.
We need a safety check on the brakes.
Wí níd a séifti chék on de bréiks.

Necesitamos chequear la seguridad del claxon/la sirena.
We need a safety check on the horn.
Wí níd a séifti chék on de jórn.

Necesitamos chequear la seguridad de la dirección.
We need a safety check on the steering.
Wí níd a séifti chék on de stíering.

Necesitamos chequear la seguridad de las paletas.
We need a safety check on the forks.
Wí níd a séifti chék on de fórks.

Necesitamos chequear la seguridad de las llantas.
We need a safety check on the tires.
Wí níd a séifti chék on de táiers.

Necesitamos realizar mantenimiento a este montacargas.
We need maintenance on this forklift.
Wí níd méintenans on dis fórklift.

Debemos retirar este montacargas de circulación.
We need to remove this forklift from service.
Wí níd tu remúv dis fórklift from sérvis.

Debemos conducir lentamente.
We need to drive slow.
Wí níd tu dráiv slóu.

Debemos utilizar nuestro cinturón de seguridad.
We need to wear our seatbelt.
Wí níd tu wéar áuer sítbelt.

Debemos chequear si la estructura rodante está en el lugar correcto.
We need to check if the rollover structure is in place.
Wí níd tu chék if de rolóuver ssstráctcher is in pléis.

Debemos chequear la alarma de marcha atrás.
We need to check the reverse signal alarm.
Wí níd tu chék de rivérs sígnal alárm

COMUNICACIONES SOBRE PELIGROS
HAZARD COMMUNICATION
Jásard comiunikéishon

Necesitamos una clase de seguridad sobre cómo utilizar la página de recopilación de datos para materiales de seguridad.
We need a safety class on how to use the Material Safety Data Sheet.
Wí níd a séifti clás on jáu tu iús de matírial séifti dáta shít.

Debemos utilizar una MSDS para cada material químico en el área de trabajo.
We need to use an MSDS for each chemical in the work area.
Wí níd tu iús an em es dí es fór ích kémical in de wérk éria.

Debemos etiquetar cada envase.
We need to label each container.
Wí níd tu léibl ích kontéiner.

Necesitamos kits de limpieza para derrames en los lugares en los que se almacenan químicos.
We need spill clean-up kits where chemicals are stored.
Wí níd spíl clín-ap kits wéar kémicals ár stórd.

Necesitamos un plan para control de derrames.
We need a spill control plan.
Wí níd a spíl contról plán.

Tenemos un plan para control de derrames.
We have a spill control plan.
Wí jáv a spíl contról plán.

Necesitamos utilizar nuestro equipamiento de protección.
We need to use our protective equipment.
Wí níd tu iús áuer protéctiv ecuípment.

ESCALERAS (MÓVILES/DE MANO)
LADDERS
Láders

Necesitamos una clase de seguridad sobre escaleras móviles/de mano.
We need a safety class for ladders.
Wí níd a séifti clás for láders.

Debemos utilizar la escalera móvil/de mano correcta para cada trabajo.
We need to use the right ladder for the job.
Wí níd tu iús de ráit láder for de chób.

Necesitamos chequear la seguridad de la escalera.
We need a safety check on the ladder.
Wí níd a séifti chék on de láder.

Debemos asegurarnos de que la escalera móvil/de mano esté limpia.
We need to make sure the ladder is clean.
Wí níd tu méik shúar de láder is clín.

Debemos marcar esta escalera móvil/de mano como dañada.
We need to mark this broken ladder.
Wí níd tu márk dís bróuken láder.

Debemos utilizar una escalera móvil/de mano de madera aquí.
We need to use a wooden ladder here.
Wí níd tu iús a wúden láder jíar.

Debemos utilizar una escalera móvil/de mano de metal aquí.
We need to use a metal ladder here.
Wí níd tu iús a métal láder jíar.

Debemos tener cuidado con los cables de alta tensión.
We need to watch out for power lines.
Wí níd tu wách áut for páuer láins.

No podemos pararnos en el escalón superior de la escalera móvil/de mano.
We cannot stand on the top of the ladder.
Wí canót stánd on de top ov de láder.

Debemos colocar la escalera móvil/de mano sobre una superficie sólida.
We need to put the ladder on a solid surface.
Wí níd tu put de láder on a sólid sérfis.

Debemos utilizar una escalera móvil/de mano más alta.
We need to use a taller ladder.
Wí níd tu iús a tóler láder.

Debemos utilizar una escalera móvil/de mano más baja.
We need to use a shorter ladder.
Wí níd tu iús a shórter láder.

EQUIPAMIENTO PARA PROTECCIÓN PERSONAL
PERSONAL PROTECTIVE EQUIPMENT
Pérsonal protéctiv ecuípment

Necesitamos una clase de seguridad sobre equipamiento para protección personal.
We need a safety class on personal protective equipment.
Wí níd a séifti clás on pérsonal protéctiv ecuípment.

Debemos utilizar nuestras gafas de seguridad.
We need to wear our safety glasses.
Wí níd tu wéar áuer séifti glásis.

Debemos utilizar nuestros protectores para el rostro.
We need to wear our face shields.
Wí níd tu wéar áuer féis shíelds.

Debemos utilizar nuestros cascos.
We need to wear our hard hats.
Wí níd tu wéar áuer járd játs.

Debemos utilizar botas con puntera de acero.
We need to wear our steel-toed boots.
Wí níd tu wéar áuer ssstíel-tóud búts.

Debemos utilizar nuestros guantes.
We need to wear our gloves.
Wí níd tu wéar áuer glávs.

Debemos utilizar nuestro arnés.
We need to wear our harness.
Wí níd tu wéar áuer járnes.

Debemos utilizar nuestra máscara para el polvo.
We need to wear our dust mask.
Wí níd tu wéar áuer dást másk.

Debemos chequear nuestras gafas de seguridad.
We need to check our safety glasses.
Wí níd tu chék áuer séifti glásis.

Debemos chequear nuestros protectores para el rostro.
We need to check our face shields.
Wí níd tu chék áuer féis shíelds.

Debemos chequear nuestros cascos.
We need to check our hard hats.
Wí níd tu chék áuer járd játs.

Debemos chequear nuestras botas.
We need to check our boots.
Wí níd tu chék áuer búts.

Debemos chequear nuestros guantes.
We need to check our gloves.
Wí níd tu chék áuer glávs.

Debemos chequear nuestro arnés.
We need to check our harness.
Wí níd tu chék áuer járnes.

Debemos chequear nuestras máscaras.
We need to check our masks.
Wí níd tu chék áuer másks.

Necesitamos reemplazar esas gafas.
We need to replace those glasses.
Wí níd tu ripléis dóus glásis.

Necesitamos reemplazar esa protección para el rostro.
We need to replace that face shield.
Wí níd tu ripléis dat féis shíeld.

Necesitamos reemplazar ese casco.
We need to replace that hard hat.
Wí níd tu ripléis dat járd ját.

Necesitamos reemplazar esas botas.
We need to replace those boots.
Wí níd tu ripléis dóus búts.

Necesitamos reemplazar esos guantes.
We need to replace those gloves.
Wí níd tu ripléis dóus glávs.

Necesitamos reemplazar ese arnés.
We need to replace that harness.
Wí níd tu ripléis dat járnes.

Necesitamos reemplazar esa máscara protectora del polvo.
We need to replace that dust mask.
Wí níd tu ripléis dat dást másk.

ANDAMIAJE
SCAFFOLDING
Ssscáfolding

Necesitamos una clase de entrenamiento sobre el armado de andamios.
We need a training class on setting up scaffolds.
Wí níd a tréining clás on séting ap ssscáfolds.

Debemos tener una clase de entrenamiento sobre los peligros de los andamios.
We need to have a training class on the hazards of scaffolds.
Wí níd tu jáv a tréining clás on de jásards ov ssscáfolds.

Debemos armar el andamiaje sobre una superficie sólida.
We need to set up the scaffold on a solid surface.
Wí níd tu set ap de ssscáfold on a sólid sérfis.

Necesitamos otra persona para que nos asista en el armado del andamiaje.
We need another person to help set up the scaffold.
Wí níd anóder pérson tu jélp set ap de ssscáfold.

Debemos colocar las barreras de seguridad.
We need to put in the guardrails.
Wí níd tu put in de gárdreils.

Debemos colocar las barreras intermedias.
We need to put in the mid-rails.
Wí níd tu put in de míd-réils.

Debemos colocar las tablas para los pies.
We need to put in the toe-boards.
Wí níd tu put in de tóu-bórds.

Debemos chequear si el andamiaje está dañado.
We need to check the scaffold for damage.
Wí níd tu chék de ssscáfold for dámich.

Debemos utilizar nuestro arnés de seguridad.
We need to wear our safety harness.
Wí níd tu wéar áuer séifti járnes.

Debemos asegurar nuestras cuerdas/nuestros cables.
We need to secure our lines.
Wí níd tu sekiúer áuer láins.

Debemos ir a buscar/coger nuestro arnés de seguridad.
We need to get our safety harness.
Wí níd tu guét áuer séifti járnes.

Debemos chequear nuestro equipo.
We need to check our equipment.
Wí níd tu chék áuer ecuípment.

Debemos realizar un chequeo de seguridad.
We need to have a safety check.
Wí níd tu jáv a séifti chék.

Debemos tener un espacio libre de 10 pies desde la línea de electricidad.
We need to have a 10 feet clearance from the electric line.
Wí níd tu jáv a tén fít clíarans from de eléctric láin.

Debemos retirar aquello del andamiaje.
We need to remove that from the scaffold.
Wí níd tu remúv dat from de ssscáfold.

¿Adónde están las tablas para los pies?
Where are the toe-boards?
¿Wéar ár de tóu-bórds?

¿Adónde están las barreras de seguridad?
Where are the guardrails?
¿Wéar ár de gárdreils?

¿Adónde están las barreras intermedias?
Where are the mid-rails?
¿Wéar ár de míd-réils?

Necesitamos más barreras de seguridad.
We need more guardrails.
Wí níd mór gárdreils.

Necesitamos más barreras intermedias.
We need more mid-rails.
Wí níd mór míd-réils.

Necesitamos más tablas para los pies.
We need more toe-boards.
Wí níd mór tóu-bórds.

ESCALERAS
STAIRWAYS
Ssstéarweis

Necesitamos una clase de seguridad sobre mantenimiento de escaleras.
We need a safety class for maintaining stairways.
Wí níd a séifti clás for meintéining ssstéarweis.

Necesitamos una clase de seguridad sobre los peligros de las escaleras.
We need a safety class on the hazards of stairs.
Wí níd a séifti clás on de jásards ov ssstéars

Debemos limpiar las escaleras.
We need to clean the stairways.
Wí níd tu clín de ssstéarweis.

Debemos mantener las escaleras libres de materiales.
We need to keep the stairway free of materials.
Wí níd tu kíp de ssstéarweis frí ov matírials.

Debemos instalar un pasamanos.
We need to install a handrail.
Wí níd tu instól a jándreil.

EXCAVACIONES
TRENCHING/EXCAVATION
Trénching/Excavéishon

Necesitamos una clase de seguridad sobre el trabajo en las zanjas.
We need a safety class for trench work.
Wí níd a séifti clás for trénch wérk.

¡No ingrese en una zanja desprotegida!
Do not enter an unprotected trench!
¡Dú not énter an anprotéktd trénch!

Necesitamos un chequeo de seguridad.
We need a safety check.
Wí níd a séifti chék.

Necesitamos darle pendiente a las paredes.
We need to slope the walls.
Wí níd tu slóup de wóls.

Necesitamos apuntalar las paredes con tablones.
We need to bench the walls.
Wí níd tu bénch de wóls.

Debemos colocar soportes alrededor de las paredes de la zanja.
We need to shore the trench walls with supports.
Wí níd tu shór de trénch wóls wíd sapórts.

Debemos proteger/cubrir las paredes de la zanja con la caja de trinchera/mula.
We need to shield the trench walls with the trench box.
Wí níd tu shíeld de trénch wóls wíd de trénch bóx.

Necesitamos otra caja de trinchera/mula para este trabajo.
We need another trench box for this job.
Wí níd anóder trénch bóx for dís chób.

Necesitamos una buena salida.
We need a good way to get out.
Wí níd a gúd wéi tu get áut.

Necesitamos una escalera móvil/de mano.
We need a ladder.
Wí níd a láder.

Necesitamos una escalera.
We need some stairs.
Wí níd sám ssstéars.

Debemos mantener el equipamiento pesado lejos del borde.
We need to keep heavy equipment away from the edge.
Wí níd tu kíp jévi ecuípment awéi from di éch.

Debemos saber adónde están bajo tierra las conexiones de servicios.
We need to know where the underground utilities are.
Wí níd tu nóu wéar de ánderground iutílitis ár.

Debemos colocarle una marca/identificar las conexiones de servicios que están bajo tierra.
We need to mark the underground utilities.
Wí níd tu márk di ánderground iutílitis.

Debemos colocarle una marca/identificar la conexión de gas.
We need to mark the gas line.
Wí níd tu márk de gás láin.

Debemos colocarle una marca/identificar la conexión de la alcantarilla/cloaca.
We need to mark the sewer line.
Wí níd tu márk de súer láin.

Debemos colocarle una marca/identificar la conexión de agua.
We need to mark the water line.
Wí níd tu márk de wóder láin.

Debemos colocarle una marca/identificar la conexión de electricidad.
We need to mark the electric line.
Wí níd tu márk di eléctric láin.

Debemos colocarle una marca/identificar la conexión de cable.
We need to mark the cable line.
Wí níd tu márk de kéibl láin.

Necesitamos una prueba del suelo.
We need a soil test.
Wí níd a sóil test.

Necesitamos una pala.
We need a shovel.
Wí níd a shóvel.